Talking & Listening

KEYS TO SUCCESS WITH CUSTOMERS AND CO-WORKERS

Instructional Design Department

Wanda J. Zeman	Project Manager
Naomi W. Peralta	Writer
Robert Klausmeier	Writer
Diane M. Lamyotte	Writer
Veronica Micklin	Writer
James E. Garner	Assistant Writer
Ruby Dau-Schmidt	Word Processing Operator
Beverly Johnson	Word Processing Operator
Gaye Matravers	Word Processing Operator

Design and Production Department

Claudia Lamm Wood	Project Editor
Jeff Davidson	Designer
Michael Tapia	Production Manager

This textbook was developed under the direction of John L. Schmidt, AIA, Vice President, and Gail Rafter Meneley, Vice President.

Institute textbooks are created under the guidance of two department directors: Naomi W. Peralta, Instructional Design, and Robert W. Brown, Design and Production.

Compositor	Impressions
Text Type	10/12 Berkeley Old Style Book

Printed in the United States of America

First Edition

01234/54321

ISBN 0-912857-52-8
Library of Congress Catalog Card Number: 89-85152

CONTENTS

PREFACE

Effective communication skills play a major role in your success in business. As an employee in a service industry, your ability to express yourself well when communicating with other employees and with customers is highly valued by your institution. Your skill at conveying ideas clearly and effectively forms a lasting impression on all those with whom you come in contact, personally and professionally.

We are not born skillful communicators. We learn to communicate in a variety of contexts throughout our lives. As working adults, the diversity and complexity of our messages require that we communicate as effectively as possible. We can improve our communication ability because communication skills can be continually developed and improved. Becoming a skilled communicator is not an easy task, but by learning the basic techniques and applying them through practice, it becomes easier.

Talking and Listening: Keys to Success with Customers and Co-Workers has been written to help employees in financial institutions improve their effectiveness as communicators in their organizations. This book is unique in its focus on the special concerns and situations faced by employees in a financial services environment. The emphasis is on communicating effectively on a professional level with co-workers, subordinates, managers and customers. Illustrations and examples drawn from the business support the concepts. Thus, you will have an opportunity to develop a clearer understanding of how to improve your own communication skills by learning about possible ways of handling interactions with others in a financial institution setting.

Your institution has confidence in your willingness and ability to represent the organization well. As a skilled communicator, you can contribute to the organization's professional image and enhance your career options as well.

Dale C. Bottom
President
The Institute of Financial Education
December 1989

ACKNOWLEDGMENTS

The Institute appreciates the contributions of the following professionals who wrote one or more chapters:

Toby Berkun, Berkun and Associates, Lisle, IL

Michael Plumpton, Chicago, IL

Rhonda S. Robinson, Northern Illinois University, De Kalb, IL

Richard C. Stern, Northern Illinois University, De Kalb, IL

Lynda Willer, University of Illinois, Chicago, IL

The Institute thanks the following individuals who contributed research or who reviewed portions of the manuscript:

Tom Darovic, Pathway Financial, Chicago, IL

Sam Downing, Brentwood Square Savings, Los Angeles, CA

Diane B. Ehrlich, Northeastern Illinois University, Chicago, IL

C. Russell Kranich, Jr., Hill Financial, Red Hill, PA

Denise Lawson, Roosevelt Bank, Springfield, MO

Barbara H. Steele, Coastal Federal Savings & Loan, Myrtle Beach, SC

Robin Thompson, Great Western Bank, Northridge, CA

Talking & Listening

KEYS TO SUCCESS WITH CUSTOMERS AND CO-WORKERS

Elliott Erwitt © Magnum Photos

"To think justly, we must understand what others mean: to know the value of our thoughts, we must try their effect on other minds."

William Hazlitt
"On People of Sense"
The Plain Speaker *(1826)*

1 Introduction to Communication

Objectives

After reading this chapter, you should be able to:

- Define *communication*;
- Explain the importance of communication to financial institution professionals;
- Describe four characteristics of communication;
- Name and explain two reasons why people communicate;
- Describe the five elements of a communication transaction;
- Explain how information is processed;
- Explain why listening skills are important to successful communication;
- Identify the four levels of human communication.

JACK WELLINGTON ASKED a loan counselor at Summit Savings and Loan, "A friend told me that if I sell my house the buyer can take over my present mortgage. Is this true?"

"If your mortgage includes an assumption agreement, yes, the new purchaser may take over your existing mortgage. Let's check your records to see if they contain this form."

"What if I just want to transfer the mortgage anyway? Can't I do that?"

"Well, no, Mr. Wellington, not without an assumption agreement. Our records show your mortgage contract contains a due on sale clause. That means that you must pay off the mortgage when the property is sold. The purchaser will be unable to assume your old mortgage, but we'd be happy to talk with you and the prospective buyer to see what can be worked out."

Jill and Melinda are two tellers at Century Savings. Because Jill has a lunch date with a friend who just flew into town, she asked Melinda to switch lunch hours with her so she could take a late lunch. "It means a lot to me," Jill told her.

"No," Melinda said. "I always take the late lunch."

"Please, Melinda, I'll return the favor for you when you need it."

"But I don't ever need it. I take my lunch the same time every day. Why should I change?"

Jill began to get angry. "Come on, Melinda. How many favors have I ever asked of you?"

"Too many," Melinda said. "I'm tired of always doing you favors."

"Well, thanks a lot," Jill said sarcastically. "I'll just have to talk to the head teller about it."

Bob Andrus, the manager of mortgage loan operations, called one of his supervisors, Joe Miller, into his office. "Joe," he said, "the people upstairs are pressing for our supervisors to learn more about the secondary mortgage market. Now, I know you may already know something about it, but a little extra training never hurt anyone. I've signed you up for a week-long seminar starting Monday."

"Well, sir," said Joe, "I wish you had told me about this earlier. I'm not sure the department will be able to spare me."

"I've talked it over with my boss, Joe, so don't worry about anything."

"But Mr. Andrus," Joe said, "we still haven't hired those two new loan counselors we need, and with that drop in the prime rate, we are just swamped with people trying to refinance their loans. I don't think I can spare the time."

"Joe, I don't think any of us are above learning something new if it will help us in our jobs. Now stop trying to avoid the issue. I'll send you all the particulars later today. Now, please excuse me; I'm late for a meeting."

What Is Communication?

For businesspeople, the ability to communicate well is critical to career success. The examples above show one successful and two unsuccessful communication efforts. Do they sound familiar? Can you describe exactly why the second two examples were communication failures and what can be done to make them succeed?

As you probably realize, communicating successfully helps us understand and be understood by others. People have an inborn need to interact with others and be understood by them. You are a social being; this characteristic affects every facet of your life, including the time you spend on the job. Your work in a financial institution consists mainly of communication—with customers, co-workers, subordinates and superiors. Communication is the means by which you interact with people. Because you work in a service business, your personal success, as well as the success of your institution, depends on your ability to convey and listen to ideas.

Although the communication process may seem simple, it is complex. Communication involves interaction between people with different backgrounds, experiences, views and ways of expressing themselves. Successful communication depends on one person conveying the message he or she intends and another person interpreting the message as intended and then responding with equal accuracy. But your own experience may tell you that this task is not easy. For example, words affect individuals differently; tone of voice and facial expression carry messages that can conflict with spoken words; and messages taken out of context can have entirely different meanings from one setting to another. Other barriers, such as differences in occupation or education, can complicate the process even further. You can reduce the effect of these barriers, and at times avoid them altogether, by learning and practicing good communication skills.

This chapter introduces the communications process. It examines the nature of communication and explores the various ways people process and exchange information. Many of the topics mentioned here, such as how to choose the most exact words and how to listen effectively, will be treated more thoroughly in later chapters of this book.

The Purpose of Communication

Why do humans communicate? You may have never asked this question because the process of communication has become almost instinctive to you. However, an awareness of the reasons for communication will help you better understand the process and sharpen your own communication skills on the job. People communicate primarily for two basic reasons: to fulfill social and psychological needs and to make decisions.

Fulfill Social Needs

People are by nature social animals. Several studies indicate that the fulfillment of social needs is essential to physical survival and mental well-being. Unless people interact with one another, they can begin to hallucinate, become physically ill, or even die prematurely.[1] This interaction does not need to involve serious, weighty matters; even simple conversation to pass the time fulfills this social need and gives people a feeling of well-being. You spend roughly one-third of your adult life in the workplace, so a major part of your social interaction takes place on the job.

Because you are a social being, you also use communication to fulfill social obligations and define your place in society. You say "Good morning, how are you?" to customers and co-workers, not because you particularly want to know the state of their health, but because it reinforces your social ties with them. You acknowledge their presence and show that you will make the effort to converse with them civilly when the need arises. By neglecting such formalities as a morning greeting, you can give people the impression that you do not care about them or wish to stay isolated from them. You may greet someone even when you do not feel particularly friendly, because you want to stay a part of the social group and are willing to go along with the social norms. Communicating with other people helps fulfill your need to belong and bolsters your sense of self.

Make Decisions

People also need to communicate to make the decisions that shape their lives. You make countless decisions every day, from what clothing to wear to work to how to prioritize your afternoon assignments. Each decision involves communicating, either within yourself or with other people. For example, to decide how to schedule your workday, you talk to your supervisor about any special assignments or problems. To determine how to help a customer make an investment choice, you need to listen carefully and gather all the pertinent background data. Since good decisions are based on correct information, you can improve your skills in decision making by becoming more accurate in your exchanges of information.

Often the decisions you make depend on the approval or cooperation of others. Consequently, your decisions will require you to influence the attitudes and behaviors of others. For example, if you want to be considered for the next promotion in your department, you need to convince your manager that you are a good candidate for the job.

IMPORTANCE OF COMMUNICATION TO A FINANCIAL INSTITUTION PROFESSIONAL

The word *communication* comes from the Latin verb *communicare*, meaning to impart or share. *Communication* is the process by which people share information about ideas, things, tasks and people through a common system of symbols, words and behavior. You transmit messages to other people—intentionally and unintentionally, successfully and unsuccessfully—every day of your life. Although communication is such an integral part of life, people sometimes lack the skills necessary to send and receive information accurately. These communication skills are important to the personal and professional life of every individual. And in service businesses, such as financial institutions, communication skills are essential. All employees should be able to give and receive information and instructions clearly, convey messages to their supervisors accurately, discuss procedures with co-workers, or describe services to customers. In every communication situation, employees who have strong communication skills are more valuable to their institutions than those who have difficulty communicating.

Communicating with Customers

Because financial institutions provide a service rather than a tangible product, they are concerned about enhancing their public image as helpful, competent service providers. This task requires employees who are skilled in listening to customer needs and complaints and in explaining the services available. In addition, the employees need to communicate—in both words and actions—their institution's commitment to serving its customers. When customers trust the institution's employees, they are more likely to believe that the institution will offer services that are in their best interest. In order to remain strong and viable, financial institutions need employees who are good communicators.

Communicating with Management

Employees also use their communication skills to deal effectively with their managers. Management often seeks employees' opinions, new ideas and suggestions that affect the day-to-day operations of the institution. Innovations and improvements in customer service often come from the employees directly involved, and effective managers strive to keep employees motivated by keeping the channels of communication open. Employees who can analyze, summarize and communicate their needs and opinions to management can have an important impact on their organization as well as their own futures with the organization.

Communicating with Co-Workers

Employees also need to communicate effectively with co-workers. Working closely with other people on a daily basis is a fact of life for most people. Whether or not this experience is rewarding depends on the communication that takes place among those people. Because you spend so much of your time at work, you will find that the effort you expend toward communicating effectively with your co-workers will help you enjoy your job more.

Working in a financial institution requires you to use your communication skills often. As you read this text, you will discover techniques to enhance your verbal and nonverbal communication skills in order to become a better communicator and a more successful and valuable employee.

Characteristics of Communication

As was noted in the opening pages of this chapter, communication is a complex process by which individuals use verbal and nonverbal symbols to share meanings and impart information. In addition to its complexity, communication is also a circular or continuous process. You constantly absorb incoming messages through your five senses. You also select, evaluate and interpret those messages in terms of your previous experience with others. And, at the same time that you receive messages, you also generate messages and send them to others. A final characteristic of communication is its irreversible nature. Once the act of communication has taken place, your message cannot be called back or altered.

Because so many factors affect the communication process, messages can be easily misdirected or misinterpreted. However, a closer look at the three characteristics of communication can help you increase your understanding of the process and sharpen your skills at sending and interpreting messages.

Communication Is Complex

To understand the complexity of the communication process, imagine if it were simple. Your listener would understand your message perfectly the first time, without the need for repetition or clarification. Similarly, you would understand every message you received. You also would be calm and confident when speaking your mind with someone or persuading someone to your point of view, knowing that your view would be understood exactly, and no further explanation would be needed.

You can see right away what a fantasy this is. Because of the differences in the people involved, no one communicates perfectly all the time. When communication occurs, it consists of a message shared among two or more individuals—the speaker, or sender of the message, and one or more listeners, or receivers. These people have different

Figure 1.1 The Communication Process

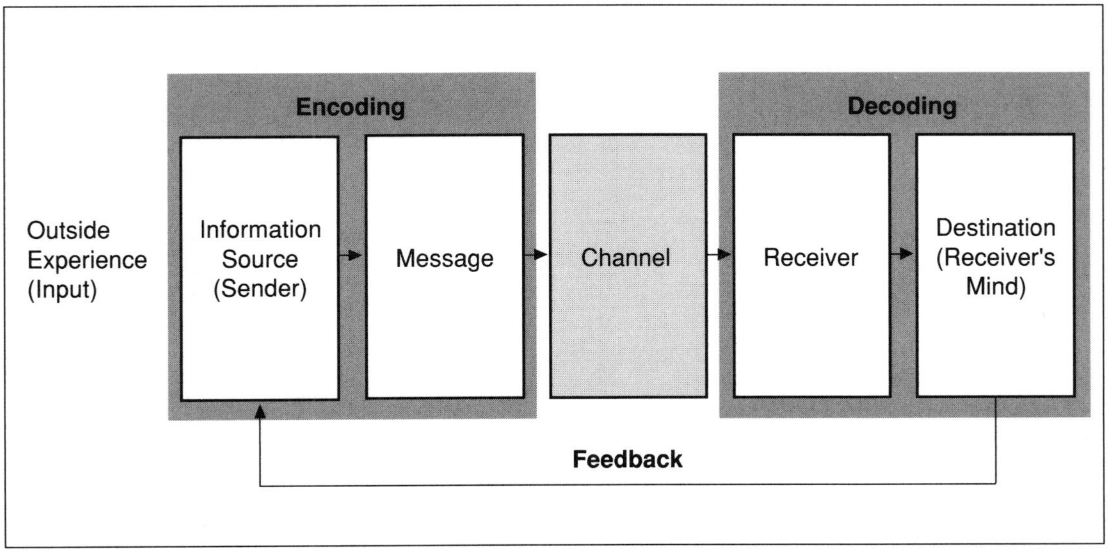

backgrounds, attitudes, education, talents, status, values, personalities, and skills in relating to others. The ability to overcome these differences determines how effectively the speaker sends the message, how well listeners receive the message intended by the speaker, and how well the speaker interprets the listeners' reactions. Every act of communication is as unique as the people involved.

Communication Is Circular

Communication involves a series of actions that results in the transmission of information from one person to another. As such, the communication process can be described as a series of give-and-take interactions or exchanges between people. The speaker must receive some response from the receiver for communication to continue. The response may be spoken words, silence, or gestures, because any of these convey a reaction by the receiver. For example, when a person smiles while agreeing to something, it indicates that the person is comfortable with that agreement. If he nods his head, it further reinforces the agreement. In this exchange, the sender interprets the receiver's gestures and determines that the original message was understood and accepted. The sender can then respond to the receiver's reactions through further words and gestures. As communication continues, both sender and receiver transmit and interpret messages from one another. This circular path is shown in Figure 1.1, which illustrates how the elements of interpersonal communication (discussed in the next section) work together to facilitate communication. Because communication is a circular process, each person in the exchange is responsible for the success of the communication.

Communication Is Irreversible

Occasionally you may wish that your thoughts had remained unsaid. Unfortunately, communication is irreversible. Once you have sent a message through a sentence or gesture, the original communication is beyond your control to call back or to alter. Even though you can rephrase or correct your statement, you cannot take back the original message. The receiver has already processed your message, interpreted it and reacted to it in some way. Even though a communication exchange is temporary, lasting only a brief time, its effects can be permanent. The better you are at sending the "right" message the first time, the less time you will spend soothing hurt feelings and clarifying miscommunications.

The Elements of Interpersonal Communication

To understand communication more fully, it is helpful to know the five elements essential to any interpersonal communication (Figure 1.1) and see how they work together to facilitate the communication process. These elements are: the sender, the message, the channel, the receiver and feedback.

The Sender

The *sender* transmits a message to the receiver. Before a message can be sent, the sender creates or selects the idea to be communicated and determines how to convey the desired message accurately via words or gestures. The process by which the sender internally converts an idea into a message is called encoding. Specifically, *encoding* is the selection and organization of bits of information into language symbols that can be transmitted to the receiver. The sender's thoughts, feelings or ideas are encoded or converted into symbols that have meaning for both the sender and the receiver. Encoding is described in more detail later.

The Message

The *message* is the expression of the ideas the sender wishes to convey to the receiver. The message can have a variety of purposes. For example, it can provide facts that a receiver may not have, change the receiver's present ideas, or request information from the receiver. It is the means by which the sender conveys an idea or initiates an action.

The Channel

The means of transmitting a message from the sender to the receiver and the route it travels is called the *channel*. In most oral communication, the message is carried both by words, which travel by sound waves, and by nonverbal signs and gestures, which travel by light waves. It is good to reinforce a verbal message with nonverbal cues, because using a greater number of channels increases the chances of successful communication. Channels are not limited to the senses of sight and sound. People communicate through all five senses. For example, think of the reassurance you feel when concluding a conversation with a strong, firm handshake.

The Receiver

The *receiver* is the person to whom the message is directed. The receiver's task is to interpret the sender's message, using as a base his or her own past experiences, expectations and culture. This process is called decoding and will be described more fully later. Although the sender may think the message is clear, the receiver determines what is received and understood. The receiver then responds to the message as he or she has interpreted it.

Feedback

The sender can check the effect the message has on the receiver by monitoring feedback. *Feedback* is the receiver's verbal or nonverbal response to the message. Feedback is the only way the sender can determine whether the message was received and understood. In oral communication, feedback occurs immediately. The sender can hear the receiver's verbal feedback before continuing the message. The sender can also notice the receiver's nonverbal reaction to the message. When the receiver nods, the sender usually interprets the nod to mean that the first part of the message was received and understood. If the receiver raises an eyebrow or appears puzzled, he or she may be signaling that the message is unclear or confusing. The sender can elaborate on or restate the message if necessary. Both sender and receiver must monitor their communication and adjust for differences in meaning to ensure effective communication.

The Communication Process

As mentioned earlier, communication is an ongoing, dynamic process of exchanging or managing information. Because of its dynamic nature, both the sender and the receiver need to respond readily and appropriately to communicate successfully. In general, each party in the communication manages information by gathering, encoding and decoding, storing, and processing it.

Gathering Information

Gathering information is the first step in the communication process. When people communicate with each other, they depend on the senses to gather information about the sender and the message. As discussed earlier, you use hearing to gather information when the sender is speak-

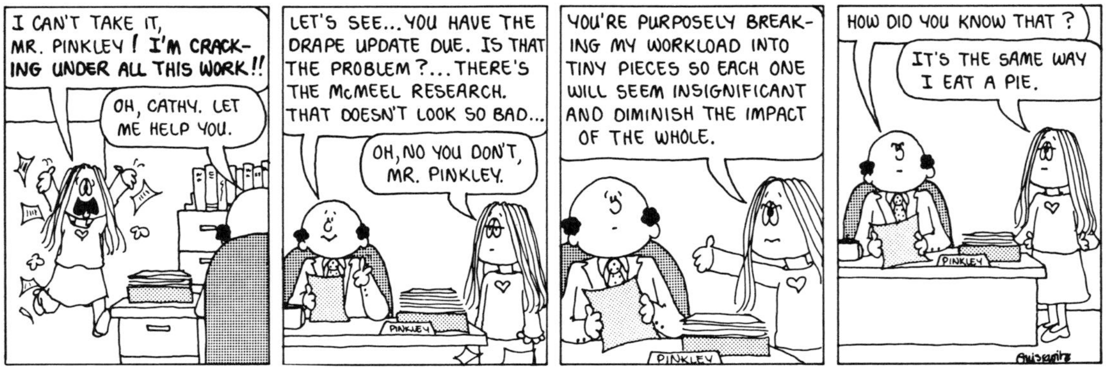

ing. Your sense of vision provides information about nonverbal cues, such as gestures or facial expressions. Likewise, the speaker's handshake or even the clothing the speaker is wearing can provide additional information. For example, people tend to think a firm handshake indicates sincerity, or that clothing that appears expensive indicates wealth. To ensure a complete, accurate message, both the sender and the receiver need complete information.

Encoding and Decoding Information

Encoding and decoding refer to the sender's and receiver's efforts to process all the information that has been gathered and transform it into usable data. As information is gathered through the senses, the sender *encodes* the information, or transforms it into meaningful symbols or codes that can be sent to the receiver. The information that is gathered has no meaning in itself. Its meaning is determined by the symbols or codes—the language—the sender applies to the information. If the sender chooses language familiar to the receiver, he or she increases the chances of being understood. If the receiver has well developed language skills and broad experience, the possibility that the message will be correctly interpreted also increases.

Because words and gestures by themselves mean nothing until people apply meanings to them, the receiver must decode the message to understand it. *Decoding* means interpreting the message from a personal viewpoint. This process requires analyzing it in light of personal history, interests, responsibilities and concerns. For example, when you first began to work in the financial services business, you may have translated some unfamiliar terms into general English to understand them. Now, with experience, these special terms are familiar to you, but you may have to interpret them for customers and new employees.

Storing Information

After a message has been sent, both the sender and the receiver store their impressions of the exchange in their memories. The receiver remembers the information conveyed in the message, including facts, opinions and personal impressions of the exchange; the sender remembers the intent and content of the message, plus the reaction of the receiver. Depending on the relevance of the message to the sender and the receiver, each may remember it for a brief period of time or for a long time. These memories will help shape every later communication between these two people.

Processing Information

People process information by making associations between new information and information already stored in their memories. Thus, when new information is processed, it is related in some way to the stored information. Information can be processed three different ways: through words, numbers or visual cues; through physical responses and emotions; and through generalized comparisons.

Words, Numbers and Visual Cues

One word can trigger a whole series of related memories or ideas. You often classify stored information according to certain key concepts, either words, numbers, or images. You then use the identifying word, number or image to recall more complex, detailed ideas. For example, if your manager asked you to prepare a report by the first of every month, you would probably remember it more easily than if it were due on the 26th of every month. Since many things may need to be done by the first of every month, such as making bill payments, the report is something to add to that list. By classifying the data by a memorable number, the entire message is easier to recall.

Physical Responses and Emotions

Many times information is linked in your memory with physical and emotional reactions. Whenever you recall that information, you will also trigger the accompanying reactions. For instance, a teller who has been robbed by a dark-haired man in a black sweater and black slacks may experience sweaty palms and increased heart rate every time a similarly dressed man approaches the teller's station. The teller has little control over these reactions because they are behavioral or physiological reactions to images or information stored in the teller's memory.

Generalized Comparisons

People's beliefs and attitudes affect their reactions to and interpretations of incoming messages. Likewise, beliefs and attitudes often determine how people remember and process messages. For example, a department manager may believe that a refusal to work overtime indicates lack of dedication. If she feels this way strongly, she may label any employee "undedicated" if, for whatever reason, he or she cannot put in additional time.

Transmitting Messages

The most useful, efficient method of sending and receiving messages is language. *Language* is a system of conventionally understood signs, sounds or gestures used to communicate ideas or feelings. Effective communicators can enhance their language skills by improving their listening and speaking skills.

Listening

In an effort to improve their communication skills, people often take college courses and adult education classes in effective speaking. Unfortunately, very few colleges or adult education programs offer classes in effective listening. Since communication is a sharing of messages between people, each party in the communication is responsible for making the communication successful. Every good speaker must also be a good listener, or else communication flows only one way.

Because they receive and distribute so many pieces of information each day, savings institution employees must be good listeners to be effective on the job. If you fail to listen to your supervisor's instructions, your mistakes and lost time will hurt both you and your institution. If you fail to listen carefully to customers' requests, your mistakes may lead them to question your competence and your institution's integrity.

Good listening takes effort and practice. Listening involves concentrating and careful thinking, which can be difficult when the person speaking is not a strong communicator. It can also be difficult because of background noise, distractions in the environment or in your own mind. For example, when you are worried about personal problems, or if you feel uncomfortable with the speaker because of previous disagreements, your listening skills are impaired.

Speaking

Speaking to strangers can be a difficult experience. Savings institution employees generally speak to a number of strangers and acquaintances every day, giving and receiving information and instructions. Because customer service is a common part of their jobs, most employees seldom think about the difficult task they are performing. Effective communicators have learned several skills to help them cope with this complex task.

Effective speakers learn to use clear, concise terms. Being concise means saying what you have to say in the fewest possible words without sacrificing completeness of the message and courtesy to the listener. When you give too much or too little information, a listener may become bored or confused. An effective communicator balances the amount of information provided so that the communication is clear and complete. For example, if a customer wants to know the interest rate for a deposit account, it may not be enough to simply state the current rate. You might answer the customer's questions about the interest rate and provide additional information about opening an account. You might also add that your institution offers certificates of deposit that pay even higher rates. By carefully observing the customer's nonverbal and verbal responses, you can determine whether you have given enough information or whether more is needed.

Relationships in Communication

You communicate differently in different relationships. The way you might speak with a friendly co-worker is different from the way you might speak at a staff meeting or with employees in another department. The feelings and attitudes between you and your listener will affect both the content and the delivery of the message. Much of a message's power depends on the people and the relationships involved in the communication. When communication takes place, at least one of four types of relationships is involved: intrapersonal, interpersonal, organizational and group.

Intrapersonal Communication

Communication that takes place within yourself is called *intrapersonal communication*. Such internal conversations allow you to make decisions and form opinions by analyzing data, either by logic or emotion. When you try to decide which job to begin first, you might mentally list the pros and cons of each job before deciding what to do. You might struggle internally with a problem, weighing each idea, compromising, sending yourself messages and choices. This inner dialogue helps you decide on your course of action. Although it may seem that no real communication takes place, you have gathered and processed information, encoded and decoded messages, and convinced yourself of one position over another.

Interpersonal Communication

The second type of communication relationship is *interpersonal communication*, or communication between two people. In this exchange of information, both people act as message senders and receivers, constantly encoding and decoding information to transmit messages to one another. Interpersonal communication allows both sender and receiver to interact with one another and to accomplish some task that confronts them.

Most oral communication in your institution will be in one-on-one relationships. Information is passed between employee and employer, between employee and customer, and between co-workers. For example, a customer may go to a savings institution to request specific information about opening a deposit account. In a positive encounter, the customer feels better because he or she received the information and was able to open an account, and the employee feels a sense of accomplishment by gaining a new customer for the institution.

Organizational Communication

A third type of communication relationship is *organizational communication*. Organizations exist to accomplish certain goals within a formal structure. As a member of an organization, you agree to perform those activities that will accomplish organizational goals. Your relationship with other employees is influenced by the common purpose you share and your interdependence on one another to accomplish the goals of the company.

Financial institutions are organizations composed of several departments, such as the accounting and mortgage departments. Although these departments may operate independently most of the time, they often join together to accomplish a goal. For example, when a loan officer is asked to approve a large commercial loan for a new shopping center development, the loan decision is not based solely on the financial information contained in the application. To determine whether the institution should grant the loan, the officer will also meet with others, including an independent appraiser, the institution's controller and a loan committee. Each participant in the process will communicate relevant information based on his or her knowledge and experience, bearing in mind the organization's goals in granting the loan. Together they will help determine whether the loan should be approved. It is the function of organizational groups to combine their skills and information to arrive at sound decisions for the institution.

Group Communication

Group communication is the fourth possible type of communication relationship. A group consists of two or more people who join together to complete a task or discuss an issue. Group communication is more complex than interpersonal communication because it brings together more people with varied experiences and backgrounds. Most groups develop a sense of team spirit or cohesiveness, which motivates individuals in the group and affects communication among group members. This team spirit can be achieved through group outings, business lunches, bulletin boards, newsletters or after-work get-togethers.

To accomplish certain goals, the institution may create specific groups or departments. For example, the complex operations of an accounting department must be handled by several people, such as clerks, bookkeepers, auditors and a controller who work together to supply financial information to the decision makers in the institution.

The function of the group is to supply both long-term and short-term information to the institution that only this particular group could supply. The unique dynamics of small-group communication are the topic of Chapter 9.

SUMMARY

People have an innate need to communicate with each other, for social reasons and for decision-making purposes. Communication is an especially important skill for people in the financial services business, who spend a great deal of their business day interacting with customers and co-workers. Your success will be greatly influenced by how well you express your thoughts and needs to other people and how well you respond to the thoughts and needs of others.

Communication is a complex, ongoing process in which people send and receive messages almost simultaneously. A person's total personality is involved during this process, including his or her background, responsibilities and values. The potential for mistakes in communication is great because so much is happening in the process and because people react to messages in uniquely different ways.

Communication is the sharing of messages between people; thus, successful communication is the mutual responsibility of the people involved. In the communication process, a speaker or sender transmits a message via one or more distinct communication channels to a listener or receiver, who interprets the incoming data and responds by words or gestures. The speaker then uses this feedback to determine whether the message was received and understood as intended, and, if necessary, provides clarification or additional information.

Raw information is the fuel of the communication process, but it must be shaped and changed so that people can use and remember it. Before transmitting a message, the sender gathers and considers the relevant information, then encodes the message so that the important data can be absorbed by the receiver. While the message is being sent, the receiver decodes it in light of personal experience and expectations. The receiver then encodes a reaction to the message that the sender must decode, completing the cycle. Both participants then process information about this exchange and store it in their memories, where it will affect future exchanges.

Effective listening is as important as effective speaking, but it can be difficult because of background noise and other factors. The manner in which messages are exchanged is determined in part by the type of relationship involved in the communication—whether it is intrapersonal, interpersonal, group or organizational. Each type of communication has a different effect on the content and the delivery of a message.

Questions

1. Define communication. Are the skills necessary for successful communication born in people or are they learned? Explain.
2. Why is effective communication important to service businesses such as financial institutions?
3. What is meant by the statement, "Communication is circular"?
4. Explain how the communication process involves a person's total personality.
5. Why is feedback important to communication? How does an effective communicator use feedback?
6. What happens when a message is encoded and decoded? Why are these processes necessary?
7. Name three ways people store information in their long-term memory.
8. Why is effective listening as important to communication as effective speaking? Why is effective listening so difficult?
9. What are the four levels on which communication can take place?
10. How is group communication different from interpersonal communication?

Footnotes

1. John Stewart, ed., *Bridges, Not Walls: A Book About Interpersonal Communication*, 3rd ed. (Reading, Mass.: Addison-Wesley, 1982), p. 65.

References

William Schultz, *The Interpersonal World* (Palo Alto, Calif.: Science and Behavior Books, 1966).

Patricia Galagan Hurley, "Supervising the Supergrad," *Training and Development Journal* (November 1984).

© Gary Guisinger/Rocky Mountain News. Courtesy Life Picture Service

"For the most part we do not see first and then define; we define first and then see."

Walter Lippmann
American journalist (1889–1974)

2 Perception

Objectives

After reading this chapter, you should be able to:

- Define *perception*;
- Explain how people's perceptions affect their views of reality;
- Briefly explain each of the three stages of perception;
- Describe how physiological factors and cultural influences affect perception, and provide an illustration for each;
- Define *self-concept* and explain two ways in which people's self-concepts affect their perception;
- Name three common tendencies that can distort our perceptions of others;
- Explain how those tendencies can create barriers to communication;
- Outline four strategies for improving perception.

WE JUST DON'T SEE EYE TO EYE on that issue." "He's got a completely different view of this than I do." "I can't get through to her; it's as if she lives in another world."

These statements illustrate one of the most fascinating and perplexing phenomena in human interaction: people have differing views of reality. Or, borrowing images from the first two statements, no two people "see" things in the same way.

Reality is a subjective concept, controlled and affected by people's perceptions. *Perception* is the process by which we make sense of our experiences. It involves gathering information through the senses and then assigning meaning to that information. We rely on our senses to provide information; we rely on our brains to organize and explain that information. Our perceptions determine our view of reality. And because people perceive things differently, they have differing views of reality.

The Power of Perception

Perceptions play an extremely important role in interpersonal relationships and in communication. Consider the following situation based on an actual occurrence in a midwestern bank.

After a recent change in top management, employees of the bank became restless and openly critical of the administration. The bank's managers were puzzled by this development, since the top management changes had not affected job functions on an operating level. No procedures or policies had changed, and the regular channels of communication were functioning as usual. After nearly coming to a confrontation with the disgruntled employees, the bank managers stumbled onto the likely reason for their employees' dissatisfaction.

On his first day, the bank's new CEO had begun a series of closed-door meetings with all the senior officers and department managers. The CEO's purpose in holding these private meetings was to get acquainted with his managers and to share his plans and hopes for the institution. All the employees knew that these closed-door meetings were taking place and wondered about them. When the employees questioned their department managers, they were told that "nothing much happened" at the meetings.

Because the new CEO and all members of management were involved, and because the meetings were held behind closed doors, the employees were not satisfied with this seemingly offhand explanation. They decided that "something must be up." As the meetings continued, the employees imagined all kinds of high-level plotting. Actions and comments previously considered routine or normal—management coffee klatches and meetings, conversations among management about recent mergers and takeovers in banks—started to take on sinister significance to the employees.

The employees began to gossip among themselves about a pending merger or takeover. Morale sank lower and lower. Because they interpreted management's silence about the imagined merger or takeover as a betrayal of trust, the employees grew sullen and uncommunicative in department meetings and in personal encounters with their department heads.

The managers knew that something was bothering the employees, but they were unaware that it was connected with their meetings. Consequently, they made no effort to explain what had been discussed in the meetings. Instead, they discussed among themselves "the employees' poor attitudes." Each group interpreted the other's attitude as unreasonable and disloyal.

The situation was finally clarified when an alert manager overheard several employees discussing the secretive meetings. As a result of this discovery, department heads called their employees together to explain the closed-door meetings thoroughly and to allow employees to air their concerns. Once the perceptions of both sides were revealed, it was possible to begin restoring cooperation and effective communication.[1]

This incident illustrates the powerful effect that perceptions can have on interpersonal relationships and communication. The problems between management and employees resulted from conflicting perceptions: each group viewed the closed-door meetings differently. An article in the *American Journal of Sociology* described how such differing perceptions can lead to misunderstandings and communication failures:

> If other people react to certain situations which are to them highly real, but are not visible to us from our point of view, we fail to understand why they behave as they do—even though, in terms of those invisible factors, their behavior is perfectly understandable and "reasonable." What really happens is that, not being aware of our own social blindness, we misinterpret (and usually denounce) their behavior as unreasonable, or abnormal or aggressive.[2]

Because perceptions are vital to our communication, an understanding of perception can sharpen our communication skills. This chapter examines the process of perception and describes factors that account for the uniqueness of each person's perception. It also explores common tendencies that distort our views of others, explains how those misperceptions can hamper communication and suggests strategies for improving perception.

The Perception Process

The process of perception begins in infancy, when we first encounter the world through our senses. As we receive stimuli through our eyes, ears, nose, skin, and taste buds, we learn to interpret these messages and begin to develop our view of reality. This perception process involves three overlapping stages: selection, organization and interpretation.

Selection

Every moment, you are bombarded by sights, sounds and smells. Because you cannot possibly pay attention to all these stimuli, you select and focus on only certain ones. Two basic factors help to determine why you focus on certain stimuli rather than others: characteristics of the stimulus and your motivations.

Characteristics of the Stimulus

Certain properties or characteristics of the stimulus cause people to notice it. Three attention-getting characteristics are intensity, contrast and movement. The more extreme or intense the stimulus, the more likely it is to catch your attention. For example, in a crowd of people, persons wearing bright colors are more likely to be noticed than those dressed in drab or soft colors. Similarly, strong or pungent odors and intense noises—such as a loud laugh or a shrill police siren—are likely to attract attention.

Stimuli that are distinctly different from or contrast with their background will also attract attention. THIS SENTENCE DEMONSTRATES HOW VISUAL CONTRAST CAN ATTRACT ATTENTION. You notice it because it looks different from the surrounding sentences. For the same reason, you will notice an individual who is dressed in a business suit when everyone else is wearing casual attire. Or you may focus on a whispered conversation in a room where most people are speaking at a normal volume.

A final characteristic that draws attention to a stimulus is movement. Through experiments with infants, investigators have learned that some receptors in the retina respond only to moving stimuli. These receptors are active only when an image moves across the visual field. A flashing neon sign, a person who abruptly leaps from his seat and a car that suddenly swerves into our path from a parking place are more likely to attract attention than if they remained stationary.

Motivation of the Individual

The selection process is also influenced by an individual's motivations. Needs, hopes and fears will direct attention to certain stimuli rather than to others. For example, a hungry person is likely to notice appetizing smells, discussions about a good restaurant or advertisements for food. A person who is walking through a deserted cemetery at night

Figure 2.1 Object and Background

may be alert to shadows, sounds or movement that would hardly be noticed in a familiar setting or during the day.

Organization

The process of organization is the second stage of perception. Once you have selected specific information, your brain arranges that information into coherent units or an intelligible order. You do not perceive the world as unstructured lines and shapes and noises. From infancy, you have learned to organize lines and shapes into people or objects; you group sounds into words or sentences or music. This process of organization helps us make sense of and interpret the information we receive. Among the numerous methods of organizing information are object and background, patterns, proximity and closure.

Object and Background

One way your brain organizes perceptual information is to classify the information as objects and background. In this method, a focal point (object) stands out from other, less distinct information (background). Figure 2.1 visually illustrates this common perceptual tendency. When

Figure 2.2 Pattern

you look at the design, do you see a series of black figures against a white background? Look at the figure again, and try to reverse the object and background so that the white sections become objects that are set against a black background. You should be able to see the word "Tiger."

With visual messages, the object and background organization sets sharply defined persons or things against a neutral or blurred background. In your work situation, for example, you will see a customer, a teller terminal or a desk as a coherent, organized whole against the less distinct area surrounding it. When this method is used with the messages you hear, you may make a customer's question or a loudspeaker announcement the "object" on which you focus, while blocking out other "background" noises.

Figure 2.3 Proximity

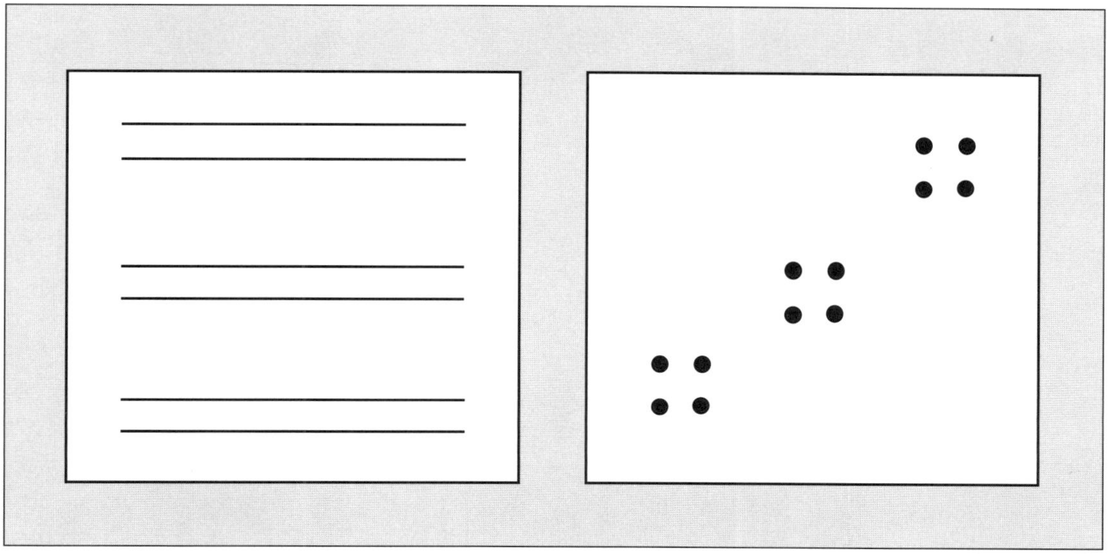

Patterns

A second method of organizing information is to look for patterns or similarities. When you organize by patterns, you group together objects that have similar characteristics. Look at Figure 2.2 for example. In the first set of objects, you may separate the figures into groups because of the similarities in the crosses and in the circles. In the second set, you may see four rows of similar shapes rather than a group of 16 individual figures.

In a similar way, when you look at a group of customers, you may organize them into subgroups on the basis of their sex (men and women), their age (elderly, middle aged, early twenties, teenagers, etc.), or the way they are dressed (business attire, casual clothes). Likewise, if you made a visual survey of your co-workers, you might group them into people who are using terminals, or people who are talking with co-workers, or people who are seated at desks.

Proximity

We also organize visual information on the basis of spatial relationships. *Proximity* is the tendency to group together those things that are located close to one another. By grouping according to proximity, we sort information into manageable pieces that are easier to remember and interpret. For example, the first illustration in Figure 2.3 probably appears to be three sets of parallel lines rather than six individual lines. The second illustration may appear to be three sets of dots rather than a collection of 12 dots.

Figure 2.4 Closure

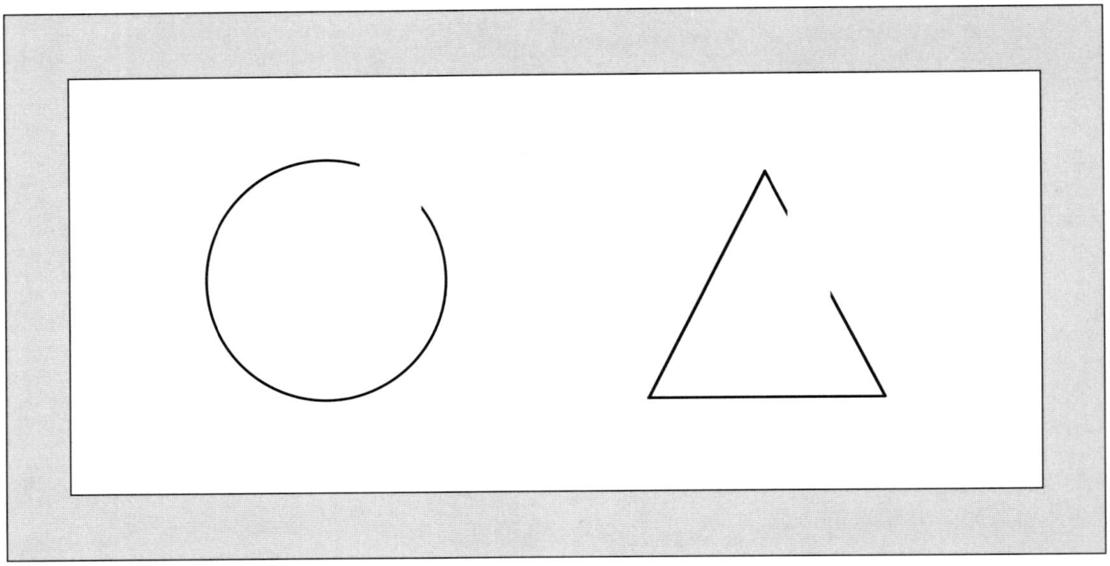

In much the same way, you use proximity when you divide the new accounts department into five interview areas instead of seeing five desks and 15 chairs. Because of proximity, you may also see the six customers waiting for loan interviews as three couples, or two couples and two singles.

Closure

A fourth technique for organizing sensory information is closure. *Closure* is the tendency to perceive information as complete even when it is not actually complete. This tendency to modify information, or "fill in the blanks," helps us draw conclusions and interpret the meaning of messages. Because of closure, you may identify the incomplete shapes in Figure 2.4 as a circle and triangle.

As an extension of this organizing principle, consider the following sentence: "When entering the building, it always necessary to punch the security code into the door keypad." The word "is" has been omitted from between "it" and "always", but as you read the sentence, your mind probably supplied the missing word, either consciously or unconsciously. This same tendency explains why you may read a road sign correctly even though part of it has been torn away, or why you may complete sentences that have been left unfinished by a speaker.

Interpretation

The third and final stage in the perception process is interpretation. After your mind has selected and organized information, it gives meaning to, or makes sense of, the information. Interpretation plays a vital role in every act of communication. To illustrate: assume that, in your role as teller, you are explaining withdrawal procedures to a customer. As you explain, the customer suddenly sighs heavily and begins to frown. You pause; his facial expression becomes the object of your attention. What do the heavy sigh and frown mean? Is he annoyed, or is he simply trying to concentrate? Your interpretation of the sigh and frown will affect the way the communication proceeds.

A number of factors influence our interpretations of sensory information. Five of those factors are past experiences, values and beliefs, expectations, knowledge of others and emotional state.

Past Experiences

Our past experiences help shape our interpretations of the information we receive. We tend to interpret each new experience on the basis of a similar previous experience. What meanings have similar events held for us in the past? How did we interpret similar information in the past? For example, consider the illustration from the preceding section: if a previous customer had frowned at your explanation of withdrawal procedures and then begun griping about the inconvenience of such "silly rules," you might interpret this customer's frown as a sign of annoyance.

Beliefs and Values

Your beliefs and values also affect your interpretation of information. *Beliefs* are those concepts that we assume to be true. People sometimes act on beliefs without testing their validity, because beliefs can become synonymous with facts in their minds. If you believe that people are generally honest, you are likely to believe your co-workers' or customers' words. If you believe that most people do as little work as possible, you will probably interpret a co-worker's explanation about his failure to complete a report as an excuse for avoiding the work rather than a legitimate reason for delay.

Values are a person's designation of certain items, principles or qualities as being worth more than others. Values identify what is important to an individual. Your values influence your interpretation of information. If decency and morality are important values to you, you are likely to form a negative opinion of co-workers who make racial slurs or tell off-color jokes. If you value hard work, you may form a favorable impression of an employee who comes to work early, frequently stays after closing, and never extends break times.

Expectations

A third factor that shapes our interpretation of information is expectations. Just as motivation influences your selection of information, your expectations color your interpretation of that information. If you believe

your supervisor is pleased with your work and may be planning to promote you, you would probably be delighted to receive a memo from her asking you to see her at 3:30 this afternoon. If, on the other hand, you sense that your supervisor does not like your work and you have heard rumors that your organization is reducing staff, the same memo may be threatening to you.

Knowledge of Others

We often base our interpretations of people's words and actions on what we have heard about those people. For example, if you know that a co-worker is experiencing marital difficulties or is about to undergo major surgery, you will interpret his silence or distant attitude differently than if you were unaware of these factors. If you have heard that your new supervisor is genuinely friendly and really likes to get to know her employees, you will be less likely to interpret her personal questions as prying or nosy.

Emotional State

A final factor that influences our interpretation of information is our emotional state or mood. Your feelings shape not only what you perceive, but how you perceive it. If you feel insecure and defensive, you may interpret a customer's remark about "all the red tape involved in a mortgage loan" as a slur on your company or even a personal insult. When you feel happy and confident, the same remark may seem harmless to you.

Interaction of the Three Stages

As noted earlier, the three stages of perception—selection, organization, interpretation—are not neatly segmented steps. The stages occur nearly simultaneously, and each stage affects the others. Your expectations or emotional state can influence not only your selection of information, but also your interpretation of that information. And your interpretations of past information will also affect your selection and organization of future data. For example, assume that a new teller once interrupted a transaction with a customer to respond to complaints from other customers waiting in line. After his response, the waiting customers became even more vocal, and the customer at his window grew annoyed about the delay. As a result of this experience, the teller decided that customers who complain in line are merely relieving tension and do not really expect him to respond. After he formed this interpretation, the teller no longer heard such complaints; or, if he did, he thought of them as background noise.

Perception is a complex process that involves a large number of interdependent factors. From this brief exploration of factors that influence the three stages of perception, you can understand why an individual's view of reality—the result of the perception process—may vary from moment to moment. The following section helps to explain why one individual's view of reality can be quite different from that of another.

Differences in Perception

Perception is an extremely personal process. Factors that influence each person's perception are particular to that individual and affect his or her perception in a unique way. Among the most important influences on perception are: physiological factors, cultural and social influences, and self-concept.

Physiological Factors

Physiological factors are related to the functioning of the body's systems for selecting, organizing and interpreting information. Because individuals differ physically, their perceptions will also differ. Some physiological factors that affect your perception are your senses, age and physical condition.

The Senses

People have differing sensory equipment. For example, some people are near-sighted; others have limited peripheral vision. Such variations in vision will result in differing visual images and, consequently, different perceptions. Similarly, variations in hearing ability will result in perception differences from person to person.

Although differences in vision and hearing are the easiest to recognize, other sensory differences exist as well. Consider your family's varying reactions to the same pot of coffee; or recall a time when you were repelled by a co-worker's new perfume. And, at one time or another, most of us have argued about room temperature—with one person claiming it is too cool and someone else insisting it is just right.

These disputes could be more than simple matters of opinion; they could be the result of differing sensory equipment.

Evidence exists that identical foods taste different to various individuals. Odors that please some people repel others. Likewise, temperature variations that create discomfort for some are inconsequential to others. These physiological factors influence the perception process and result in differing views of reality.

Age

A second physiological factor that influences the perception process is age. Developmental differences that occur at different ages can affect perceptions. The Swiss psychologist, Jean Piaget, described a series of developmental stages that children experience on their way to adulthood. On the basis of experiments, Piaget discovered that younger children are unable to perform certain mental tasks that come naturally to adults.[3] For example, until about the age of seven, children cannot assume another person's point of view. Because they assume that everyone else feels the same way they do, young children may, at times, seem selfish or uncooperative.

Age can also be an indirect factor in differing perceptions among adults. As previously described, past experiences affect the way people select, organize and interpret information. Older people who have had a wider range and number of experiences than those who are younger may also have different processes for selecting, organizing and interpreting sensory information. People's age may also affect the functioning of their senses of vision, hearing, touch, smell and taste.

Physical Condition

A final physiological influence on perception is your physical state. Poor health or fatigue may cause you to select, organize and interpret sensory information in a different way than you might normally and, consequently, to perceive things differently from someone who is feeling good or is well rested.

Can you recall a time when you struggled through work with a bad cold or after a sleepless night? Generally, under these conditions, thought processes slow down and the level of tolerance decreases. As a result, you may miss important sensory information—such as a co-worker's passing greeting or a customer's smile. Or you may be quick to interpret your supervisor's query about the cash drawer totals as a challenge to your abilities or the accuracy of your work.

Cultural Influences

In addition to physiological factors, cultural influences can result in differing perceptions among people. *Cultural influences* include the customs, traditions, beliefs, values and attitudes that characterize a particular social group. Some of the many cultural groups to which you may belong include your family, your work group, your friends, your community, your nation. Even though many of these groups overlap, each culture contributes distinct ways of viewing the world.

Cultural influences can create differences in perception among co-workers in the same financial institution. Humor, for example, is strongly affected by culture. Jokes that are considered funny in one person's ethnic group may be interpreted as offensive to co-workers of a different ethnic group. Different cultures also have different perceptions of time and timeliness. What is "on time" in one person's family or nationality may be considered inappropriately early or late in another's.

Over time, your financial institution and the department in which you work have developed customs, traditions, beliefs, values and attitudes that form a unique corporate or department culture. This culture will also influence the perception process and may result in perception differences among workers or between employees and customers. The longer you work with an institution, the greater the likelihood that the corporate or departmental culture will influence your perceptions. If your institution places a high value on being "financially aware," for example, you may find yourself becoming more alert to news reports, headlines, and conversations in which financial news is discussed. If your department stresses courtesy and respect for the customer, you may discover that you listen more keenly for expressions of politeness and react negatively to indifference or rudeness in co-workers or friends. If your institution stresses accuracy and careful money management, you may form a negative impression of customers who are careless or indifferent about balancing checkbooks.

Finally, the culture of our society influences our perceptions by the roles it prescribes for the sexes. From early childhood, we are taught—directly and indirectly—roles that are appropriate for men and women. Until recently most people never questioned the roles that our society assigned to men and women. Men were to be strong, independent, aggressive, competitive, risk-taking breadwinners. Women were to be passive, empathic, fragile, dependent, noncompetitive mothers and housewives.

During the past 20 years, groups concerned about equal opportunity and fair treatment for both sexes have questioned these traditional roles. As a result, some of the stereotypes and traditional roles have begun to erode. Despite these beginnings toward a more open and fair assessment of the sexes, however, traditional cultural stereotypes still influence many people's feelings about sex roles.

Your own attitudes toward sex roles are determined by the various cultural groups that have formed your beliefs and values. These attitudes

Reprinted by permission of UFS, Inc.

affect your perceptions of interactions with others. For example, if you have been taught to believe that men should be strong and aggressive, you may interpret a male supervisor's display of compassion as a sign of weakness. On the other hand, a co-worker whose view of male and female roles is less traditional may interpret the same display as a sign of strength.

Self-Concept

A powerful influence on perception is the self-concept. *Self-concept* is a kind of a mental mirror that reflects how you view yourself. This "mirror view" includes all aspects of your being: appearance, intelligence, physical capabilities, talents, likes and dislikes, emotional states. Your self-concept is your understanding and awareness of your unique qualities.

Individuals' concepts of themselves influence their perceptions of events and other people. We often view others in the same way that we view ourselves. Extensive research indicates that persons with positive self-concepts are likely to think well of others, whereas those with negative self-concepts will probably have low opinions of others.[4] Likewise, people with poor self-images often tend to interpret personal and world events from a cynical, pessimistic perspective, whereas people with positive self-images have more optimistic outlooks.

To better understand how self-concept influences perception, it is helpful to know how our self-concepts are formed and how they function in the perception process.

How the Self-Concept Is Formed

Although your self-concept can be altered and enhanced throughout your life, most of its development occurs before you reach adulthood. Three factors influence the formation of the self-concept: your self-appraisal, the reactions and responses you receive from other people, and the roles you play in life. Although these factors are interdependent and often overlap, each can be examined separately.

Self-Appraisal *Self-appraisal* is your definition of yourself based on what you see and what you have experienced. For example, you may stare at yourself in a mirror and make a mental list of physical characteristics: brunette, tall, slightly overweight, clear complexion. On the basis of how you feel about what you see, your list will also include judgmental ingredients such as "nice smile," "well-groomed," "good taste in clothes."

Other elements of a self-appraisal, such as your abilities (athletic, good reader, good cook), likes or dislikes (travel, parties, meeting new people), will be the result of your reactions to your experiences. For example, if school was easy for you, you might add "intelligent" or "fast learner" to your list. If you receive satisfaction from your job as a bookkeeper, you might add "enjoys working with numbers."

If you conducted a self-inventory and included as many items as you could, your list might contain hundreds of descriptive terms. The ability to recognize which of the terms are most important to you and to know which characteristics best describe your essential self is an important part of self-appraisal.

Reactions and Responses from Others In addition to your own impressions of yourself, the reactions and responses of others with whom you communicate also help to form your self-concept. The amount of attention and affection you received as a child, the kinds of compliments you received, the questions and comments you heard about your behavior all influenced the development of your self-concept. For example, if your parents always told you that you had a "short fuse," you may grow up believing yourself to be short-tempered. If your teachers and classmates always complimented you on your clothes and personal grooming, you may see yourself as well-groomed or stylish. If friends frequently comment on your regular attendance at church or synagogue, you may come to think of yourself as religious.

Others' messages about your appearance, beliefs, abilities, moods and mannerisms all affect your self-concept. You use such messages to reinforce, adjust or validate your view of yourself. And the more you respect the people who send the messages, the more weight you will give to their comments and reactions. If the messages are positive and complimentary, your self-concept is likely to improve or to remain positive.

The Roles You Play Finally, the roles you play help to form your self-image. Think about the various roles you have assumed in life. Your list could include child, student, spouse, parent, employee, friend, neighbor, entertainer, listener, church member, and so on. Even if you limit the list to your workplace, you should be able to name quite a number of roles: employee, teller, problem-solver, good listener, information source, co-worker.

Some roles are chosen by the person who plays them. For example, you may decide to pattern yourself after a friend who is a good listener or after a thoughtful, sincere supervisor you work for. Or you may assume the role of style setter after several co-workers have complimented you on your clothes or makeup.

However, some roles are imposed on you by groups to which you belong. Your family, your friends, your co-workers and your church help determine your roles by approving or disapproving of what you say and how you act. They mold you into a certain kind of person when you are with them, and you begin to see yourself in that role. To illustrate: your friends may see you as the life of the party, and you accommodate them by playing that role—even when you are tired or bored or depressed. Your co-workers may assign you the role of news source, and you find yourself spending more and more effort finding out the latest information from the office grapevine.

No matter how you acquire roles, they will affect your image of yourself. And how you feel about those roles and the way you play them will help determine whether your self-concept is positive or negative.

Functions of the Self-Concept

With the recent popularization of psychology in best-selling books and on radio and television shows, the term "self-concept" and some of the above information about how the self-concept is formed may already have been familiar to you. You might be surprised, however, at the dynamic nature of your self-concept and the influence it has on your process of perception. Self-concept influences perception in two important ways: it filters the information you receive, and it helps determine your interpretation of that information.

Information Filter Your self-concept often acts as a filter for messages that other people send to you. You choose to hear and pay attention to those messages that support or reinforce your image of yourself and ignore or disregard those that do not. For example, consider a teller who sees herself as a model employee. She graciously accepts compliments from the people around her, including her supervisor and customers. If, during a staff meeting, the supervisor mentions her in a list of tellers whose cash drawer totals have not balanced, the teller may not even hear her name, or she may ignore what she heard, thinking that the supervisor made a mistake. If, however, the teller sees herself as a poor worker or careless employee, she may come into the meeting expecting to hear her name on such a list.

Likewise, an employee who sees himself as a style setter may be alert to some employees' admiring stares or compliments about his trendy new suit, while overlooking raised eyebrows or chuckles from other employees who find the suit wild or outlandish.

This filtering process may seem to contradict earlier information about how the comments of others influence our self-image. However, your self-image both affects and is affected by others' comments. This process is cyclical: some comments by others will help develop a self-image that, in turn, filters comments that do not agree with that image. When some new comments do penetrate the filter, the self-concept is altered and begins a new filtering process.

Information Interpreter A second important function performed by the self-concept is to interpret information. Your feelings about yourself or the image you have of yourself will influence the way you assign meaning to the messages you receive. To illustrate how people's self-concepts affect their interpretation of messages, consider the following situation: Mitch and Luisa are loan processors in the main office of a large financial institution. Mitch feels highly confident of his abilities and skills in the lending department. He also considers himself a real go-getter, and is hoping to maneuver his skills into a promotion soon. Luisa, on the other hand, feels very insecure about her skills and often wonders whether she would be better suited for a different position in the institution. She sees herself as a follower and thinks she might be happier in a less responsible position.

One morning, Jim Fischer, the lending department supervisor, calls both Mitch and Luisa into his office. "We've been doing a lot of thinking about revising our residential mortgage lending procedures," he tells them. "I'd like the two of you to take charge of an evaluation committee that will come up with suggestions for streamlining and improving our current procedures."

Mitch is delighted with the assignment. He sees it as a display of his supervisor's confidence in him and an affirmation of his skills and abilities. He also sees the assignment as Fischer's possible way of testing his readiness for that hoped-for promotion. Luisa is appalled by the assignment. She views it as a threat and an invitation to failure. She wonders why Fischer is picking on her. Does he think she doesn't have enough to do? Or is he just hoping she will really botch up so he can finally get rid of her?

As a result of their self-images, these two employees interpreted the same message very differently. In a similar way, a person who considers herself a popular co-worker and friend might interpret another employee's joking comments as an invitation to camaraderie, while some-

Reprinted by permission of UFS, Inc.

one who sees himself as the outsider in the group might find such comments insulting or hurtful. Because the self-concept is a powerful influence in the process of perception, people will generally go out of their way to interpret messages and information in a way that will support their image of themselves.

Mistaken Perceptions of Others

As you have seen, physiological factors, cultural influences and the self-concept play important roles in determining our perceptions of the world around us. Because all these influences affect individuals differently, each individual's process of perception and resulting view of reality will be unique. Such differing views of reality can pose barriers to communication between individuals. One final communication barrier related to the perception process is our tendency to form incorrect impressions of others.

When we interact with other people, we form impressions of them. These impressions are our views of what they are like—or their "reality." All of the factors discussed previously play an important part in determining our perceptions of other people. In addition to these factors, however, our perceptions may be colored by three tendencies that can distort our judgment and our perceptions. Such distorted perceptions frequently lead to problems in relationships and in communication among people. These tendencies are: assuming others are like us, being swayed by first impressions, and stereotyping.

Assuming Similarities

When people meet others who are similar to them in age, gender, profession, race and income level, they frequently assume that the others are also similar to them in personality, attitudes and motives. If you are a customer service representative who loves your job and respects the supervisor, you will probably assume that your co-workers also love their jobs and respect the supervisor. On the other hand, if you are not happy with your job and enjoy griping about your supervisor's "unfairness," you may assume that your co-workers feel the same way. This tendency to perceive others as we do ourselves is similar to the phenomenon that psychologists call "projection," in which people project their own attitudes and feelings onto others. The following situations illustrate some of the barriers to communication that may result from this tendency:

- Jim has never liked the branch manager of his institution. He enjoys hearing negative comments or snide jokes about the manager. Because he assumes that his co-worker, Lucille, feels the same way he does, Jim tells her the "latest dirt" on the manager. Lucille is offended by the story and begins to avoid Jim.
- Carlos lost his temper over a mistake made by Jennie, the bank's new receptionist, and made some rude comments to her. Later, he felt bad about the remarks. He knew that if Jennie had said things like that to him, he would refuse to talk to her. Consequently, Carlos has avoided her for several weeks. Jennie, on the other hand, was disgusted with her mistake and felt that she deserved the criticism. Noticing that Carlos is avoiding her, Jennie assumes that he is disgusted with her. As a result, she tries to stay out of his way.

As these examples illustrate, the tendency to assume similarities between ourselves and others is often a mistake, and it can lead to serious communication problems.

Being Swayed by First Impressions

The second tendency that can lead to mistaken perceptions of others is labeling people according to our first impressions of them. We form first impressions of people as a natural part of the perception process. After we have met someone for the first time, we leave with such impressions as "He really knows his stuff" or "What a grouch!" or "She seems like a lot of fun."

Our first impressions often determine how we will respond to people in our future interactions with them. For example, if your first impression of a co-worker is "He really knows his stuff!" you may listen carefully to what he says, respect his opinion, and come to him for advice or answers. Once we have formed an opinion of a person, we tend to hold on to that opinion and make any conflicting information fit the image we have of him or her.

Problems can arise, however, if your first impressions are inaccurate. As previously indicated, a number of factors may contribute to a faulty or unfair perception in a first meeting. The new person may be in a rare good mood or feeling particularly confident because of a recent promotion; or he may be under stress or not feeling well. Similarly, your own mood or physical condition may result in a faulty first impression.

When we continue to cling doggedly to these first impressions, we tend to judge every interaction with the person and interpret every message in a way that supports those impressions. If we persist in such behavior, our first impressions can become self-fulfilling prophecies. In other words, if you continue to react and respond to your co-worker as though he were a grouch, he is quite likely to become a grouch when he is with you.

Stereotyping

A third tendency that can distort our perceptions of others is stereotyping. A *stereotype* is a generalization and a judgment about an entire group without regard for individual differences in the group. We are especially prone to stereotyping when we do not know a group well. For example, a person from the Midwest who has never had much contact with Californians but has read about several people from California who eat health foods, spend a lot of time on the beach, and have an easygoing attitude toward life, may assume that all Californians are "health nuts," "beach bums" and "laid back." Or, if you know several librarians who are quiet and intelligent and who love to read, you may stereotype all librarians this way. Then, if an ex-librarian comes to work at your institution, you may decide—even before you meet him—that he is quiet, intelligent and a book-lover.

Stereotyping creates problems for two reasons. In the first place, stereotypes are usually inaccurate. And in the second place, they prevent you from getting to know a member of a group as a unique individual. Consider the barriers to communication created by a person's stereotyped perception of elderly people in the following work situation.

Art Bellton is a customer service representative at County Federal Savings Bank. He looks up from his desk and smiles as he sees Lettie Burke, an elderly customer, approach. Art stands and greets Lettie in a friendly but overly loud voice: "Good morning. I'm Art Bellton. Please have a seat. How may I help you?" As Art moves to help Lettie into the chair he has pulled out, Lettie brushes away his offer of assistance and seats herself.

"There's no need to shout. My hearing is excellent. I'd like to apply for a home improvement loan," she says.

Art smiles and leans toward Lettie, remembering to speak in a softer voice. "Planning to dress up the place so you can sell it?" he asks. "I'd be happy to help you out. And maybe I can also interest you in some of our trust services—for the grandchildren, you know."

Lettie fixes Art with a cold stare before responding. "As a matter of fact, Mr. Bellton, I *don't* plan to sell my home. I'm getting married soon, and I'd like to do a little remodeling before my new husband moves in. And I'm not interested in your trust services; I don't have grandchildren, you know."

IMPROVING PERCEPTION

You have studied some of the many factors that can influence and color the process of perception. You have also discovered ways that the perception process varies from person to person. And you have seen how these differences and our distorted perceptions of others can create problems in communication.

How can you improve your skills in perception and become a more effective communicator? The following four tips can help you analyze and improve your own process of perception:

- understand that people have different perceptions;
- identify potential causes of misperceptions in order to avoid them or lessen their impact;
- learn to separate fact from inference;
- check the accuracy of your perceptions.

Understand That People's Perceptions Differ

As obvious and simplistic as it may seem, an essential first step toward improving your perception skills and your skills as a communicator is to recognize that people have differing perceptions. Your view of reality is not the same as that of your supervisor or co-worker or spouse or friend. Most of this chapter has been devoted to an examination of some factors—value judgments, beliefs, attitudes, emotions, self-concept—that account for these differences. Our perceptions cause us to see the world not as it is, but as we need or would like to see it.

Once we understand how the perception process colors our view of reality, we can begin to see why co-workers or supervisors might not see eye to eye with us on a particular issue or why they might have a different view of the problem we are discussing. This awareness can help us feel less threatened by challenges to our views, increase our openness to differences and disagreements, and encourage us to reevaluate our own perceptions.

Identify and Avoid Causes of Misperceptions

By now, you are aware that your perceptions of people and messages are not always accurate. As you read about the factors and tendencies that can lead to faulty perceptions, you may have recognized ones that you are particularly influenced by or prone to. If you can identify the influences that often distort your own perception, you may be able to avoid them or at least reduce their effect. For example, if you know that your first impressions of others have a powerful influence on future interactions with them, you can make a conscious effort to remain open-minded and willing to change those impressions as future interactions prove you wrong. If you know from experience that your perceptions are often inaccurate when you are fatigued or anxious, you can be more critical of these perceptions.

Learn to Separate Fact from Inference

Facts are verifiable data about what we have observed. *Inferences* are the conclusions we draw on the basis of what we have observed. Both facts and inferences play a part in the perception process. As you select, organize and interpret information, you will often draw conclusions or make inferences on the basis of incomplete information.

As an illustration of how facts and inferences operate in perception, consider the following situation: From her teller station, Julie watches a man wearing a large-brimmed hat, a trench coat and dark glasses enter the bank. He pauses in the lobby and glances around the bank, staring at the tellers, the other customers, and the security guards standing near the door. As the man walks toward Julie's station, he pulls his hat down low over his eyes and raises the collar of his trench coat, covering much of his face. Just as he approaches Julie, the man reaches into the pocket of his trench coat and begins to pull out a dark, metallic-looking object. Julie has been watching the man since he entered the bank. The description above contains the facts that Julie has observed. If, on the basis of these facts, Julie hits the silent alarm button, she will have made an inference on the basis of incomplete information. She will have concluded that the man is about to rob the bank.

Julie's interpretation of what she observed may be true, but it may not be; or it may be only partially true. For example, the man actually may have been trying to conceal his identity in order to avoid someone he had seen, and not because he intended to rob the bank. The dark, metallic-looking object that he began to take from his pocket may have been a pipe or eyeglass case. In that case, Julie's inference would not only have been wrong, it would have led to a rather embarrassing situation for Julie, the customer and the institution.

There is nothing bad about making inferences. We must make inferences in order to give meaning and sense to our experiences. However, problems can arise when we fail to distinguish between facts and inferences or when we jump to conclusions by assuming that our inferences are facts.

Check the Accuracy of Perceptions

Misunderstandings and communication problems often arise when we act on our perceptions without bothering to verify whether we are correct. By double-checking what you think someone said or meant, you can avoid confusion or misunderstanding.

One method of verifying your perception of verbal messages is paraphrasing. In paraphrasing, you use your own words to express the message that you have heard. This technique allows the speaker to correct any misinterpretation and gives him or her the impression that you are really trying to listen to the message. Another technique to check perceptions is to ask others for their interpretation of messages. Comparing your view of an incident or message with the opinions of others will help you understand how they perceive the same situation.

Future chapters in this book describe additional techniques that can help you check the accuracy of your perceptions and better understand the perceptions of others. In addition, the text offers suggestions about careful use of words, an understanding of nonverbal communication, listening skills, and the use of empathy—all of which can help you improve your perception and correct misperceptions.

SUMMARY

Perception is the process of making sense out of experiences. Understanding how you and other people perceive the world is an essential step toward improving communication. The more you know about the process of perception, the better able you are to interpret communication situations and to communicate effectively with others.

The perception process involves three stages that overlap and occur almost simultaneously. When you encounter information through your senses, your brain selects, organizes and interprets that information. The process of selection is influenced by characteristics of the stimulus such as intensity, contrast and movement, and by your own motivation or emotional state. After you have selected sensory information, your brain organizes it into an intelligible order, using methods of object and background, patterns, proximity, and closure.

The final stage in perception is assigning meaning to the information. Five factors influence your interpretation of information: your past experiences, your beliefs and values, your expectations, your knowledge of others and your emotional state.

A number of factors account for differences in perception among people. Physiological factors such as sensory equipment, age or physical condition can cause people to perceive things differently. Cultural influences can also result in varying perceptions among individuals. A final and important factor that creates differences in perception is the self-concept.

The self-concept reflects how you view yourself. People form self-concepts through self-appraisal, reactions and responses of others, and the roles they play in life. The self-concept influences perception by filtering information and by coloring the interpretation of that information. You tend to select only information that supports your view of yourself, and you interpret that information to agree with your self-concept.

Three common tendencies often distort our perceptions of others. We frequently assume that others are like us; we are often swayed by our first impressions of people; and we frequently stereotype groups or individuals on the basis of incomplete information. Such tendencies prevent us from seeing differences in individuals, and they create major barriers to effective communication.

You can improve your perception skills and become a more effective communicator by understanding some of the reasons why people's perceptions differ. By accepting these differences, you can become more open to other people's views and more critical of your own. If you can identify some of the tendencies that frequently distort your own perceptions, you can reduce their effect. By learning to separate fact from inferences and by checking the accuracy of your perceptions, you can improve your communication skills and avoid possible confusion and misunderstanding.

Questions

1. Define *perception*. Explain how people's perceptions affect their view of reality.
2. Briefly describe the three stages of perception.
3. List five factors that influence the interpretation of sensory information and give an illustration for each.
4. Give two examples each to illustrate how physiological factors and cultural influences can create differences in perception among people.
5. Define *self-concept* and briefly explain the three factors that influence its formation.
6. Name two ways that the self-concept influences perception and give an example to illustrate each.
7. List three tendencies that can distort your perceptions of other people. Explain how each can result in communication barriers.

8. What are four tips that can help to improve perception skills?
9. Explain how two of those tips can make you a better communicator.

FOOTNOTES

1. Paul Preston and Thomas Zimmerer, *Business: An Introduction to American Enterprise* (Englewood Cliffs, N.J.: Prentice-Hall, 1976), pp. 123–125.
2. Gustav Icheiser, "Appearances and Realities: Misunderstanding in Human Relations," *American Journal of Sociology*, Vol. 55 (1949), p. 111.
3. Jean Piaget, *The Origins of Intelligence in Children* (New York: International Universities Press, 1952).
4. P. Baron, "Self-Esteem, Ingratiation, and Evaluation of Unknown Others," *Journal of Personality and Social Psychology*, Vol. 30 (1974), pp. 104–109.

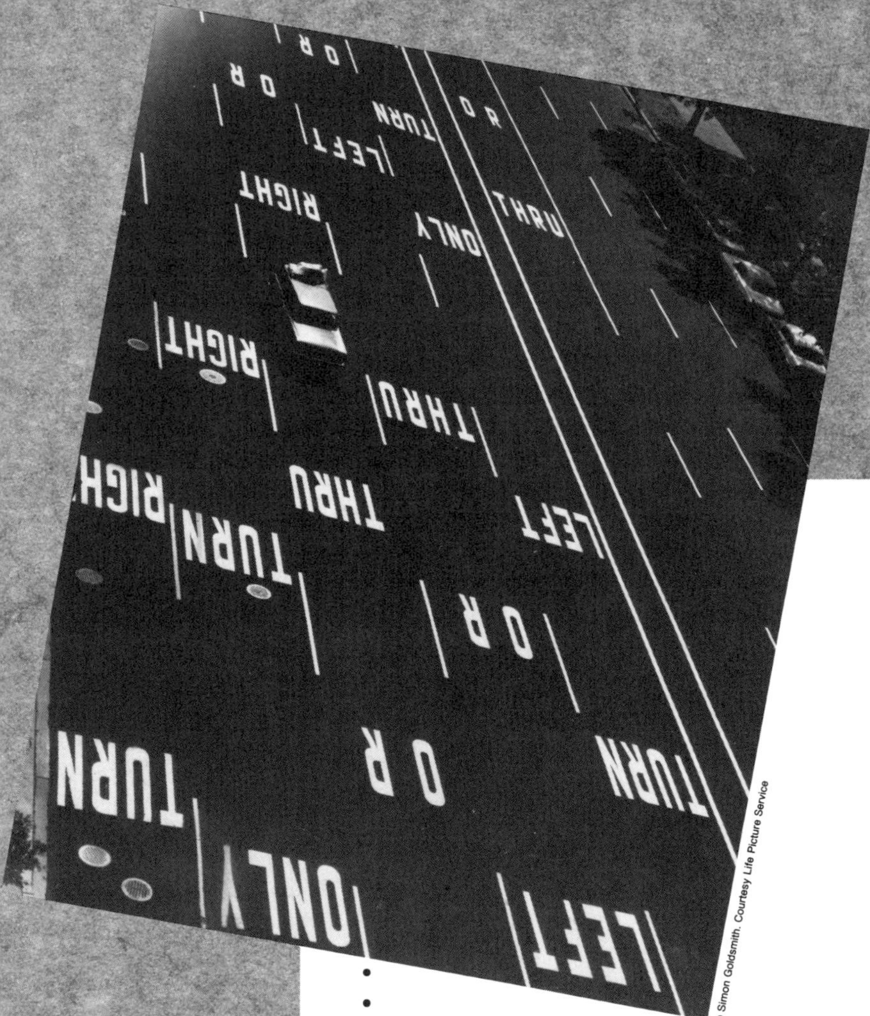

© Simon Goldsmith. Courtesy Life Picture Service

"There is always time to add a word,
never to withdraw one."

Baltasar Gracian
The Art of Worldly Wisdom *(1647)*

3 Use of Words

Objectives

After reading this chapter, you should be able to:

- Explain what is meant by the *denotative* and *connotative* meanings of words;
- Give an example of the denotative and connotative meanings of two words that you commonly use;
- Define *context* and explain how a word's meaning is affected by context;
- Identify three factors that influence a person's choice of words;
- Explain how relative and abstract language can create communication problems;
- Give an example of loaded language and explain how it can cause barriers to communication;
- List five techniques for improving verbal skills;
- Define *dating* and *indexing*, and explain how these techniques can increase the accuracy of language.

WORDS HAVE POWER. They are the means by which we transmit information and create messages. By your choice of words, you can include or exclude, praise or condemn, clarify or confuse. Your skills as a communicator depend to a large extent on your ability to use words effectively.

Your choice of words affects your relationships with supervisors and co-workers and influences customers' feelings about your institution. For example, which of the following statements has more power to inspire customer confidence in your institution? "We've got an insuring agency to cover most of the money deposited in our institution, so you don't really need to worry about your account," or, "Your funds are completely safe with us; your account is insured up to $100,000 by an agency backed by the full faith and credit of the U.S. Treasury." If you chose the second statement, you know that specific, factual information can help reassure a customer about account safety.

The more you understand about the power of words and the effective use of language, the more skillful you will become at communicating. This chapter examines the importance of language, its components and structures, factors that influence word usage, and techniques that you can use to improve your verbal skills.

NATURE OF LANGUAGE

Language is any system of symbols used uniformly by a group of people. English, mathematics and Morse code are all languages because they are composed of symbols that conform to certain rules. By themselves, words have no meaning; only when people agree to relate a certain word to an object, feeling or concept do words gain any meaning. For example, if you ask a customer to use a pen to sign a withdrawal form, the customer knows that you do not want her to sign the form with the three-letter word that has the sounds *p*, *e* and *n*. You mean that she should use an instrument for writing in ink—an instrument that is symbolized by the word "pen." The word "pen" merely expresses or symbolizes your meaning; the word "pen" is not itself the meaning. It is only by common agreement that we can understand the meanings of words and use them effectively.

Just as people need to agree on which words to attach to objects or events, they also need to use those words according to agreed-upon rules. If not, a sentence would be nothing more than a jumble of unrelated symbols that conveys no idea. Two types of rules govern language usage: syntactic rules and semantic rules. *Syntactic rules* indicate how words can be arranged to form phrases and sentences. They include elements such as grammar and punctuation.

Semantic rules govern the meaning of words in the context of sentences. Generally, semantic rules identify how individuals respond to a particular word. Despite general consensus, people can still hold different meanings for the same word, based on their perceptions and backgrounds. For example, "ARM" will have a different meaning to a loan officer than to a security guard. Generally, words have two kinds of meanings: denotative and connotative.

Denotative Meaning

Denotative meaning is the dictionary definition of a word, indicating how people will generally use the word. However, this general agreement on meaning does not ensure universal understanding of a word for several reasons. First, words can have many definitions; second, meanings change over time; and third, meanings of words are affected by the context in which the words are used.

Words Have Many Definitions

Through time and usage, a single word can develop numerous definitions. In fact, the 500 words we use most commonly in everyday communication have more than 14,000 dictionary definitions.[1]

The word "bank" for example, has at least 12 dictionary definitions, including an establishment for receiving, lending or issuing money; a steep slope, as of a hill; and a bench for rowers of a galley. The word "bank" is often used as a general term for all financial institutions despite the distinctions between commercial banks, savings institutions and credit unions. "Bank" can also be used as a verb, as in, "I bank at Quality Savings and Loan," or even, "You can bank on it."

Meanings Change over Time

Another reason denotative meanings do not ensure universal understanding is that word meanings can change over time. For example, the meaning of the term "savings account" has changed in recent years. It used to mean exclusively a passbook savings account. Now the term "savings account" can also mean a certificate of deposit or a money market deposit account. Thus, two people could use the same words and mean different things. Communication can break down when people use words with outdated meanings. A generation gap can arise when people of one age group do not understand the new meanings another age group has given to old words. Because individuals of varying ages interact in the workplace, it is important to be aware of changes in word meanings over time.

Meanings Are Affected by Context

A third reason denotative meanings do not ensure universal understanding is that meanings of words are affected by the context in which the words are used. The *context* is the relationship the word has with other words in the message. A phrase pulled out of a conversation may not have the same meaning it had in the context of the whole message.

For example, one department head might say to another, "We'll have to tighten our belts and cut back on bonuses this year, but staffing will remain at present levels." If you overheard only the first nine words, or only the words "cut back," you would probably think that layoffs in your department were imminent.

Context not only affects the meaning of a word, it can also provide clues to help you decipher a word's meaning. Often an unfamiliar word can be made clear by the rest of the words in the sentence. For example, if someone were to say to you, "Our supervisor is so obstinate; you can't budge him an inch when he thinks he's right," you could correctly assume that "obstinate" means "stubborn," even if you had never heard the word "obstinate" before.

Context can also refer to the situation in which the message is shared—where it takes place, the reason for it, the people involved, and so on. If a department head said to a colleague, "I think we'll have to cut back," he most likely is offering an opinion. If he made the same statement at a board meeting, his statement would be less an opinion and more a recommendation. If he said it to one of his employees, he might be conveying a decision.

The context in which words are used gives messages more meaning than the individual words that compose the message. To understand the meaning of words, consider the context in which they are used.

Connotative Meaning

Although you generally rely on denotative meanings in your use of words, human communication also involves other subtle and more variable word meanings. As your perceptions develop during your lifetime, you begin to associate words with memories, situations and emotional states. You begin to communicate more fully when you pay attention to the associations between words and the emotions they arouse. *Connotative meaning* is the emotional content or impact of a word. In other words, connotative meanings are the feelings and attitudes that come to mind when you choose a word or hear a word. These reactions are based on your past experiences with that word. Because everyone's experiences differ, words have different connotative meanings for every individual.

Some words, such as "the" and "it," have no connotative meanings. But a word such as "bankruptcy" may have a strong emotional impact on someone who has an overextended credit limit and is seeing a financial counselor. Likewise, the word "customer" has different connotative meanings to employees in accounting and to employees who have direct customer contact. Someone in accounting who has little personal interaction with customers may interpret the word "customer" as an abstract person "out there." A teller, who has daily contact with the public, might associate "customer" with specific individuals. Additionally, if a teller enjoys working with people, the word "customer" will carry more positive feelings than it would to a teller who does not enjoy working with people.

Because words have both types of denotative and connotative meanings, you need to be aware of both types of meaning as you choose your words. Words with strong emotional power can color and change a conversation—and often create unintended communication barriers. For example, if you were describing a co-worker's thoroughness and attention to details, you might choose to call him "detail-oriented" or "picky." Although both descriptions have similar denotative meanings, "detail-oriented" has neutral or positive connotations while "picky" has negative connotations. Depending on your listener's feelings about the co-worker, the description you choose may affect the conversation either positively or negatively. Similarly, if you wanted to encourage careful saving and spending habits with a customer, you would be wise to choose such words as "thrifty" or "frugal" rather than "penny-pinching" or "tight-fisted," even though all four terms have similar denotative meanings.

Influences on Language Choice

Knowing that words can carry more meaning than their dictionary definitions is the first step in improving your command of language and of communication. Your reasons for choosing certain words depend on cultural and subcultural influences and individual influences. Consequently, your language choices reveal who you are and the social forces that have shaped you.

Cultural and Subcultural Influences

Language choice depends in part on the cultures and subcultures in which people are raised and to which they still belong. In a society as culturally diverse as the United States, this concept is especially important. If two people speak different languages, one English and the other Spanish, communication may not be possible without an interpreter. But differences can occur even when the same language is spoken. For example, Oriental people who speak English may prefer to use ambiguous terms and to avoid direct statements. In Eastern language and culture, people express thoughts more figuratively than most Westerners do.[2]

Subcultures within organizations and groups also influence language usage. A subculture is a group within a culture, differentiated by characteristics such as age, status and gender. Within the culture of your savings institution, subcultures could include the various departments, management or nonmanagement personnel, and employees or cus-

Reprinted by permission of UFS, Inc.

tomers. Language differences among subcultures exist for a variety of reasons. Often a particular subgroup needs a specialized language to conduct business. Think, for example, of your own department. When you communicate with other members of your department, you probably use different words than you would to communicate with other departments in the institution. You may use abbreviations or terms that have meaning only within the department and would need a fuller explanation to be understood by outsiders.

Subcultures also create language differences to establish their own identity. Examples include "inside" jokes, slang and unique names for common procedures. Although these devices may make it easier for department members to communicate with each other, they can create confusion or misunderstandings in communication with people outside the department.

Individual Influences

Your choice of words also involves personal factors. Individuals bring unique characteristics to the communication process, and these characteristics play an important part in determining word choice. Among these personal factors are occupation, size of vocabulary and self-esteem.

Occupation

Occupations can influence the words people choose and the way they use those words in conversations. Words frequently used in the workplace are often assimilated into everyday conversation. Imagine that you overheard the following fragments of conversations. Try to guess each speaker's occupation.

- I think we could access his information if we can input the right data and catch him in a receptive mode.
- Jerry wouldn't get passing marks as a conversationalist. He doesn't know the first thing about subject/verb agreement, and his speech is full of dangling participles.
- I'm feeling especially illiquid just now. I'm also out of checks for my NOW account. Until my PIN arrives in the mail I can't draw cash from the ATM. It's like I've got a check hold on all my funds.

Did you guess a data processor, an English teacher and a financial institution employee? Although the examples are exaggerations, they illustrate some ways that our occupations can influence our speech.

Size of Vocabulary

One of the most obvious influences on word choice is the size of a person's vocabulary. The larger your vocabulary, the greater the pool of words you have to choose from. People such as writers and editors, whose skill in using words is essential to their occupation, frequently have a vocabulary of 40,000 words or more. College students may have vocabularies of from 10,000 to 30,000 words. However, some scholars claim that the average American's vocabulary is shrinking because people are spending more and more time watching television than reading books, newspapers and magazines.[3]

Self-Esteem

People's attitudes about themselves affect their choice of words. People with high self-esteem are more likely to use language that reflects confidence, authority and responsibility. For example, people with high self-esteem tend to make statements that reflect direct ownership of feelings or opinions: "I am happy to have you as a friend," rather than "It's good to have you as a friend," or, "I want to change this procedure," rather than "This procedure ought to be changed." People with high self-esteem also are less likely to disguise opinions and feelings in the form of questions. They would not say, "Are you having trouble with these new withdrawal forms?" when they mean "I am having trouble with the new forms," or, "Don't you think the new manager is great?" when they mean "I like the new manager."

Conversely, people with low self-esteem may betray their poor opinions of themselves by an excessive use of qualifiers in their speech.

Instead of making clear, concise statements, they add such phrases as "I may be wrong, but . . ." or "Now this might not be the way you feel about it, but . . ." Such word choices can result in communication problems. Imagine how a supervisor's authority could be undermined if she introduces a new procedure by saying, "Now I'm not sure this is going to work, but . . ." Or think how an employee's explanation of deposit account features could lose credibility if he qualifies his descriptions with expressions such as "maybe," "I guess," "kind of," or, "don't quote me on this, but . . ."

Common Types of Misleading Language

Words that carry multiple or vague meanings often cause communication problems. If you are aware of the misunderstandings such words can create, you may be able to avoid using them, or at least reduce the confusion they cause. Language can be misleading when it is equivocal, relative, loaded or abstract.

Equivocal Language

Equivocal language means language that can be interpreted in a number of ways. Poets, cartoonists and punsters often use equivocal language to make a point or evoke a chuckle. For example, in describing the outcome of a race in which a favored competitor came in second because she tripped over her own feet, a punster might say of the winner, "She won that race by a foot." In daily communication, however, equivocal language can cause problems.

Imagine the confusion that could result from the equivocal language in the following illustration. John Thomas comes into a financial institution to ask for his first loan. He is somewhat nervous as he meets with Ted Frazier of the loan department. As proof of his creditworthiness, John shows Ted his paycheck stubs, his insurance policy and his credit card balance. After Ted has looked over these materials, John offers to show him letters from various people, stating that he is a good credit risk. However, Ted declines this offer. "I don't need to read those," Ted explains. "The material I've already seen is enough to determine unsecured credit for you."

Because John is nervous, and because he is unfamiliar with loan terminology, he interprets this statement differently than Ted intends. John thinks that the words "unsecured credit" and the refusal to read the letters mean that Ted considers him a bad risk and that he is refusing to give him credit. If Ted had anticipated this misunderstanding, he might have worded his explanation more clearly: "I don't need to read the letters; the other material indicates that you are a good enough risk to get credit without collateral." By avoiding the equivocal words "unsecured credit," Ted could have saved John some anxious moments.

Relative Language

Many words, especially adjectives, have relative meanings; that is, their meanings are determined by comparison with other words. Words such as "fast," "slow," "large," "small," "better" and "worse" gain worthwhile meaning only when they are paired with an easily measured standard. You can use such words as "large" or "small" to describe your financial institution, but these words become meaningful only in a comparison with other institutions' physical size, assets, number of employees, etc. Likewise, a supervisor would not be offering helpful guidance merely by telling an employee, "Your work is getting better." To provide meaningful information, the supervisor needs to include some standards of comparison: "You've had far fewer errors in your cash drawer balances during the last few months, and your cross-selling record is now one of the three best in the department."

Loaded Language

Loaded language comprises words that elicit a strong emotional response. Misunderstandings can occur when people fail to consider the emotional power tied to the words they use. For example, consider the following conversation in which two employees discuss their supervisor.

> ***Max:*** Wow! Did you see the way Pam stood up to the manager about the proposed changes in vacation schedules? I never would have believed it! That woman is really pushy!
>
> ***Alice:*** What do you mean "pushy"? When Tom was supervisor, he used to stand up to the manager all the time. You never called him pushy. You thought he was tough and aggressive. You've just got a problem because Pam's a woman. Sexist!
>
> ***Max:*** Hey, wait a minute! I don't know what you're talking about. I wasn't running Pam down. You sure are touchy!

What just happened? The conversation degenerated into a name-calling session because of loaded language. The word "pushy" triggered the problem because it elicited a strong negative reaction in Alice. If Max had been more sensitive to the emotional power of words, he might have chosen to describe Pam as strong or tough instead of pushy. Alice's subsequent use of "sexist" and Max's accusation that Alice is touchy reduce the likelihood that effective communication can be restored to this conversation. The use of loaded language can create real communication problems.

Abstract Language

Abstract words refer to general concepts, people or places. Words such as "work," "person," "car" or "financial institution" are examples of abstract words. *Concrete words* refer to specific concepts, people or places. "Loan counselor," "Donna Miles," "Ford Escort" and "Johnstown Savings Bank'' are examples of concrete words. Semanticists have developed an *abstraction ladder* to show the progression of words from most abstract to most concrete.[4] The following abstraction ladder illustrates words that refer to your place of employment.

- The financial institution business (most abstract)
- A savings and loan association
- Midtown Savings
- The customer service division of Midtown Savings
- The new accounts department of Midtown (most concrete)

The use of abstract language can create communication problems. If your choice of words is too abstract, your message may be so vague that your listener does not understand what you mean. Consider the following comments made by an employee to a customer:

- Before you can make a deposit to your account, you'll need to fill out one of *those forms over there.*
- Your deposit will be credited to your account within *a few days.*
- You can make make deposits after you get off work, because *we've got evening hours three nights a week.*
- We need *some information on your employment history.*

When you choose abstract words to convey your meaning, you may be inviting confusion. Note how much clearer the above examples become when the abstract words are replaced with concrete words.

- Before you can make a deposit to your account, you'll need to fill out one of *the green deposit slips located in the rack near the door.*
- Your deposit will be credited to your account within *three working days.*
- You can make deposits after you get off work, because *we are open until 9 p.m. each Monday, Thursday and Friday evening.*
- We need *the names and addresses of all your employers during the past five years.*

Techniques to Improve Verbal Skills

The previous material provided a basic introduction to the use of words and the role they play in communication. The more you know about the nature of words and their power to evoke varying responses, the more effectively you can communicate. In addition to this background information, here are a number of practical guidelines to help you sharpen your verbal skills.

Build Your Vocabulary

As was previously noted, the larger your vocabulary, the greater the pool of words you have to choose from. You can increase your vocabulary by reading newspapers, magazines and books regularly. Keep a dictionary nearby to look up the meanings of unfamiliar words. Make these new words part of your working vocabulary by using them in conversation. Also, if you hear an unfamiliar word, ask the speaker to explain the meaning, or first try to infer it from the context in which it is used.

Know Your Listeners

In addition to being clear, the words you use must be appropriate to your listeners. Who are the people you generally interact with on your job? How much do you know about the backgrounds, interests and needs of your customers and co-workers? The more you know about your listeners, the better equipped you are to choose words they understand and feel comfortable with. Customers who are not employed in the financial services business may not understand technical words and specialized language that are familiar terms to you and your co-workers. Likewise, jargon and abbreviations that simplify communication within your department may create confusion for new employees or employees from other departments.

Employ Feedback

You can check to see that your choice of words is appropriate to your listeners by eliciting feedback from them. Feedback can be as simple as periodically asking questions: "Is anything unclear to you so far?" "Do you have any questions?" "Do these procedures make sense to you?" You might also look for nonverbal feedback—such as facial expressions and gestures—to determine whether or not your listeners understand your message.

Consider the Setting

The setting in which communication occurs is an important factor in determining word choice. Most people have one vocabulary for talking with family members, another for socializing with friends and a third for conversing at work. For example, a person might use off-color humor among friends but not when talking with family or with customers at work. Communication problems can arise when you use vocabulary that is inappropriate to the communication setting. Most financial institutions wish to convey an image of trustworthiness, authority and friendliness to their customers. Consequently, in your on-the-job communication, you will want to choose words that reflect this positive image. Conversely, you will try to avoid language that can detract from the image your institution wishes to convey.

Compare the Unfamiliar to the Familiar

You can often clarify your message by making comparisons. When explaining unfamiliar terms or procedures, you might refer to a similar term or procedure that your listener is familiar with. For example, instead of merely listing the features of your institution's money market deposit account, you could compare its features to those offered by a regular checking account. Once the customer realizes the similarities, he or she can better understand the additional features of MMDAs and more easily weigh the benefits they offer.

Use Examples

By using examples, you can help eliminate confusion caused by vague or abstract words. Instead of telling a customer that your institution offers "several transaction accounts that would suit your needs," add specific examples: a NOW account, a Super NOW account, a money market deposit account. The addition of these examples makes the term "several transaction accounts" less vague and clarifies your explanation. Likewise, in explaining loan procedures to a customer, you can clarify an expression such as "we will need to check your references" by listing the specific reference checks that are involved: employment history, savings account records, credit bureau reports.

Use Dating

The accuracy of information is often affected by the passing of time. Data that are accurate today may be outdated tomorrow. For example, the accuracy of the following statements is subject to change as time passes: "The interest rate on fixed-rate mortgages is 10%." "More customers are opening deposit accounts than taking out loans." "The new teller has trouble balancing his cash drawer."

To make statements like these more accurate, you can date your information. *Dating* means adding a time reference to indicate when

Reprinted by permission: Tribune Media Services.

the given information was true or when currently true information may change. By dating the above examples, you can increase their accuracy and eliminate possible misunderstanding: "As of today, the interest rate on fixed-rate residential mortgages is 10%; however, this rate is subject to change with the market." "During the first six months of this year, more customers were opening deposit accounts than taking out loans with our institution." "On Monday and Tuesday of this week, the new teller had trouble balancing his cash drawer."

Use Indexing

All of us generalize when we use what we have learned from one experience and apply it to another. For example, a teller who discovers that several customers respond favorably to a friendly greeting may decide to offer a friendly greeting to all of her customers. The teller has generalized on the basis of her experience. Generalizing can create communication problems, however, when we fail to take individual differences into account. For example, a bookkeeper tells his co-worker, "Watch out for problems with the new auditor; I worked with a guy from that firm last year, and his work was really sloppy." Such a generalization is misleading because it disregards the possibility that other employees of the auditing firm may be careful workers.

To avoid misleading generalizations, you can use the technique of indexing. *Indexing* is the practice of acknowledging individual differences. It helps eliminate the tendency to make generalizations that may not be true. The bookkeeper could index his statement to make it less misleading: "I worked with an auditor from that firm last year, and his work was really sloppy; but I'm sure that not all their auditors are careless. If they send a different person this year, you may not have any problems."

Notice how the following generalizations are made more accurate by indexing:

> ***Generalization:*** Most of my customers like to get several dollars in small change when they withdraw cash. It's always a good idea to include some silver when you dispense cash for withdrawals.
>
> ***Indexed:*** Most of my customers like to get several dollars in small change when they withdraw cash. So it's a good idea to keep plenty of silver in your cash drawer in case your customers ask for change. But you'd better check with them first, because some customers want only bills.
>
> ***Generalization:*** Mrs. Malone almost always cashes her Social Security check on the third of the month. Today is the third, and here comes Mrs. Malone. You can start reaching for the cash drawer.
>
> ***Indexed:*** Mrs. Malone almost always cashes her Social Security check on the third of the month. Today is the third, and here comes Mrs. Malone. But just to be on the safe side, you'd better check with her before getting out the cash. She may decide to deposit her check today.

Summary

Words are powerful communication tools. Your skill as a communicator can be enhanced if you understand the nature of words and their power to evoke varying responses.

Human language is a system of symbols—including words—used uniformly by a group of people to communicate. The use of language is governed by syntactic and semantic rules. Syntactic rules include such elements as grammar and punctuation that determine how words are arranged into phrases and sentences. Semantic rules govern the meaning of words in the context of sentences.

Words have two types of meaning: denotation, which is a word's dictionary definition, and connotation, which is the emotional power or impact of a word. In choosing your words, it is important to be aware of both their denotative and connotative meanings.

A person's choice of words is affected by cultural and subcultural influences, and personal factors such as occupation, size of vocabulary and self-esteem.

Language can be misleading when it employs words that are equivocal, relative, loaded or abstract. Language is equivocal if it can be interpreted in a number of ways. Relative words such as "large" or "better" derive meaning only by comparison with other words. Loaded language can cause misunderstandings because of the strong emotions it arouses. Words that are vague or abstract may fail to communicate effectively.

You can sharpen your verbal skills by following eight practical guidelines:

- Increase the size of your vocabulary.
- Know your listeners and use words appropriate for them.
- Get feedback by asking questions of your listeners and observing their gestures and facial expressions.
- Choose language that is appropriate to the setting.
- Clarify the meaning of unfamiliar words by comparing them with words your listener knows.
- Use examples to eliminate confusion caused by abstract words.
- Use dating to make your statements more accurate.
- Use indexing to avoid misleading generalizations.

CHAPTER QUESTIONS

1. What is the difference between the denotative and connotative meaning of a word?
2. Give an example of a word that has different denotative and connotative meanings and explain how this difference in meaning might create communication problems.
3. What is context? Explain the importance of context to understanding the meaning of words.
4. How does culture shape word choice? Give two examples to support your answer.
5. List three personal factors that influence word choice. Supply an illustration of how one of these factors can influence choice of words.
6. What is relative language? Explain how it can create communication problems.
7. Give two examples of loaded words and explain how these can hamper communication.
8. Name and briefly describe five techniques for improving verbal skills.
9. Supply a concrete example that clarifies each of the following abstract terms: loans, accounts, transactions, customers, alternative mortgage instruments.

10. Define *dating* and *indexing* and explain how these techniques can increase the accuracy of language.

Footnotes

1. Ronald B. Adler and George Rodman, *Understanding Human Communication* (New York: Holt, Rinehart & Winston, 1988), p. 52.
2. Kathleen S. Verderber and Rudolph F. Verderber, *Inter-Act*, 4th ed. (Belmont, Calif.: Wadsworth, 1986), p. 231.
3. Verderber and Verderber, p. 59.
4. Adler and Rodman, p. 65.

"The reality of the other person is not in what he reveals to you, but in what he cannot reveal to you. Therefore, if you would understand him, listen not to what he says but rather to what he does not say."

Kahlil Gibran
Arabic writer and artist (1883-1931)

4 Nonverbal Communication

Objectives

After reading this chapter, you should be able to:

- Define *nonverbal communication*;
- Explain the relationship between verbal and nonverbal communication;
- Analyze specific kinesic behavior to determine the possible nonverbal message;
- List and describe four characteristics of nonverbal messages;
- Explain how the use of space affects human communication;
- Define *paralanguage* and explain its importance to communication;
- Explain how the value and meaning of time affects communication.

MUCH OF YOUR CAREER SUCCESS depends on how well you use language to communicate. Language is a systematic means of conveying ideas or feelings through commonly understood signs, sounds, gestures or marks. Verbal messages can sometimes be ambiguous, incomplete or difficult to grasp, since verbal communication depends solely on words and sounds. Although you rely heavily on verbal language, nonverbal language accounts for more than half of all communication between people. Thus, people communicate as many ideas or feelings nonverbally as they do verbally. A walk, gesture, smile or frown communicates a message to other people. However, you do not have to perform an action for nonverbal communication to take place; your lack of movement may also send signals to others. For example, you convey messages by the clothes you wear, the work space you occupy or the accessories with which you surround yourself. Regardless of your intentions, you constantly communicate nonverbally with other people.

Often nonverbal messages—a stroke of the chin, a hand over the mouth, a tug of an earlobe—can announce that what you are saying and what you are feeling are two different things. But, since body language is highly visible, it can often aid communication by reinforcing the underlying message.

FUNCTIONS OF NONVERBAL COMMUNICATION

Any communication that occurs without the use of words is called *nonverbal communication*. Nonverbal communication functions in at least four ways. First, nonverbal communication can either complement or contradict what you say. When nonverbal communication complements what you say, it reinforces your message and gives it added credibility. However, if it contradicts or conveys a message that is different from the one that is spoken, it weakens the message and diminishes its credibility. For example, when your supervisor smiles warmly and says, "Great work," you can be reasonably certain that he or she is pleased with your performance. However, if the words are accompanied by a frown or a look of disgust, you might assume that the supervisor is being sarcastic.

Second, nonverbal communication can substitute for words. Most people understand that moving one's head from side to side means "no" and that moving it up and down means "yes." Nonverbal communication can effectively substitute for words only when the people involved apply the same meaning to the nonverbal message.

Third, nonverbal communication regulates the flow of communication between the sender of a message and the receiver. When receivers nod their heads in agreement, the sender learns that the message has been received and understood. If, however, the receivers look puzzled, the speaker learns that the message was not understood. He or she might then repeat the message or add an explanation. In these ways, the nonverbal cues provide the speaker with information about whether to continue, modify the message or stop talking.

Fourth, nonverbal communication can accentuate certain words or phrases. For example, in an informal conversation, you might use your fingers to make imaginary quotation signs in the air to indicate that what you have just said is a quote from someone else or a word with more than one meaning. Or you might indicate the relative size of an item by using your hands. Your gesture often clarifies your message.

Interpretation of Nonverbal Communication

A nonverbal communication can convey several different messages. For example, if a teller supervisor winks after making a statement, some tellers will believe the wink means, "Don't believe what I just said." Other tellers might understand the wink to mean, "We're all in this together." Still others might interpret the wink as a nervous habit that has nothing to do with the verbal message.

When an employee is late for work consistently, he or she sends a nonverbal message to the employer. The employer can interpret the message that the employee does not care much for the job. Another possible interpretation might be that the employee does not feel regulations—such as starting times—are important. Whatever the intended message, the actual message received by the employer depends on the employer's interpretation. Thus, nonverbal messages are open to interpretation, which varies depending on the receiver's skill and experience and the circumstances surrounding the communication.

Characteristics of Nonverbal Communication

Although nonverbal communication seems widely varied, all nonverbal communication has several characteristics that distinguish it from other forms of communication. The following characteristics apply to all nonverbal communication.

1. Interpretations determine meaning.
2. Nonverbal communication may be intentional or unintentional.
3. Actions speak louder than words.
4. Nonverbal communication provides clues about the sender.
5. Circumstances affect the meaning of the communication.

Reprinted by permission of UFS, Inc.

Interpretations Determine Meaning

As demonstrated earlier, nonverbal communication can have different meanings to different people. These differences can exist because of varying ages, cultures or backgrounds among people. Just as words must have certain understood meanings for communication to take place, nonverbal cues need to hold the same meanings to the people involved.

For example, you are supervising a new teller and someone asks you how the person is working out. You might give a signal of "thumbs up," because you like the new teller and things are going smoothly. If the other person is unfamiliar with this gesture, however, he or she could interpret your meaning in a different way, or even think you have given the new teller the "heave-ho."

May Be Intentional or Unintentional

People often send out nonverbal communication whether they know it or not. One leading authority estimates that nonverbal communication provides 65% of the informational cues people use to communicate.[1] Several studies have concluded that, despite attempts to control your nonverbal communication, people will unintentionally send messages.

Speakers often use tone of voice, gestures and facial expressions to send intentional nonverbal messages. When a customer lowers his or her voice, leans toward a loan officer and looks around quickly before beginning a conversation, the loan officer can conclude that the customer is intentionally supplying cues about the importance of this conversation. All the nonverbal messages indicate that the customer wants to guard the privacy of the ensuing conversation.

On the other hand, some nonverbal messages are unintentional. General body postures can provide valuable clues about communication. People are not always fully conscious of body stance, but it may provide clues about the spoken message. For example, if on a crowded plane you sit quietly reading a book, you avoid communication with fellow passengers. Although you do not verbally indicate that you wish to be alone, your posture communicates this message to others. Your posture provides a *cue* or signal that tells others that you do not wish to be disturbed. Therefore, even inaction communicates your mood or intentions to others nonverbally.

Actions Speak Louder Than Words

Nonverbal communication carries a message independent of—and often stronger than—a spoken message. For example, if a customer twitches, shifts his weight and looks at the ceiling while attempting to cash a check, the message, "Don't bother to check my balance; this check is good," need not be vocalized; the nervous behavior conveys the message. These nonverbal messages could indicate something is bothering the customer and the teller would be wise to check the account balance, the signature card and the check itself to determine whether the check should be cashed.

Nonverbal messages can actually contradict the accompanying spoken messages. When actions and words seem to conflict, people tend to place more confidence in the message communicated by action. If your supervisor walked by your desk and said offhandledly, "Nice work on that report," but through tone of voice and gesture remained aloof, he or she unintentionally delivers a negative message. However, if your supervisor sat down at your desk to say, "Nice work on that report," you would probably think he or she studied the report carefully and was giving a sincere compliment. Most people believe that, although a person may learn to deceive with words, the accompanying gestures will betray that person's true intent. If you want to become a more effective communicator, a greater awareness of your nonverbal cues will prevent you from unintentionally impeding or detracting from your spoken message.

Provides Clues about the Sender

Just as dialect and diction can indicate a great deal about geographic roots, certain gestures or choice of clothing also provide important clues

"A general! Goodness gracious, you don't look like a general!"

about an individual. For example, if a customer sits calmly and makes effective, natural gestures, the savings counselor may conclude that she is relaxed and confident. A smile and pleasing manner additionally indicate that the customer is comfortable and at ease.

Choice of clothing, an important type of nonverbal communication, is critical to the first impression formed of a person. A business suit sends the message, "I'm a professional who is worthy of your trust," and so it is the dress code for most financial service professionals. If the suit is wrinkled or dirty, however, a customer or employer may be unable to see beyond the employee's apparent sloppiness to the employee's abilities.

Circumstances Affect Meaning

Events or circumstances influence any communication. As you learned earlier, meanings of words vary among people and can affect how well people communicate. If certain words connote the same meanings for both the speaker and the listener, then communication is easier and more effective. For example, the word "work" may mean "security, fun, fulfillment" to one person, but "entrapment, boredom, drudgery" to another. Therefore, when two people attempt to discuss their work, their previous work experience, their values, their goals and other factors affect their communication. When they agree that work is pleasant, both probably interpret the word "work" similarly. The circumstances that precede their communication enable them to communicate.

Circumstances surrounding a situation also affect nonverbal communication. You might think that certain gestures, such as a pat on the back, would have the same meaning in all situations, especially without any words to accompany it. But a pat on the back could evoke very different reactions between two men, or between a man and a woman; between two peers, or between a superior and a subordinate; after a compliment, or after a rebuke.

In all cases, the circumstances surrounding the communication influence the transmission, reception and interpretation of verbal and nonverbal communication. Words and gestures are usually selected to convey a particular meaning. Since meaning can be misinterpreted, you need to pay attention to your listener's reaction to determine whether your messages are interpreted as you intended.

For example, Michael is a construction loan manager for a savings institution in a small but growing suburb. In that less formal atmosphere, Michael's habit of taking off his jacket and rolling up his sleeves before making a presentation at a board meeting conveyed to other people his "roll up your sleeves and get to work" attitude toward getting his work done. If Michael worked for a more formal institution in the downtown business district, this same action might seem out of place or, worse, be interpreted as disrespect or sloppiness.

Elements of Nonverbal Communication

Nonverbal communication is composed of several elements of complex parts. Tone of voice, physical surroundings, body posture and body movements—all of these convey a message. Elements of nonverbal communication include proxemics, body motion or kinesic behavior, touching behavior, paralanguage, artifacts, the communication setting, and time.

These elements reinforce or contradict verbal communication. Listening only to the spoken word can distort messages, and observing only the nonverbal cues can also create confusion. Carefully combining both verbal and nonverbal cues enhances communication. Researchers have conducted studies in these areas to determine what nonverbal messages mean. This section of the chapter summarizes much of the findings of this research and places it in the context of the daily operations of savings institutions.

Proxemics

With the increased popularity of the phrase "personal space," many people have an increased recognition of the importance of spatial relationships to nonverbal communication. *Proxemics* is the study of personal space. It examines the nature, degree and effect of the spatial separation that individuals tend to maintain. Communication is prohibited, inhibited or enhanced by the distance between the people who are communicating. Architecture, room design and the arrangement of surrounding objects are other spatial elements that influence communication. The study of how people use space in communication is often divided into environmental space and personal space.

Environmental Space

In totality, our *environment* comprises the circumstances, objects or conditions that surround us. The study of proxemics focuses on the space created by the environment, both by architecture and physical objects, identified respectively by Edward Hall as fixed-feature space and semifixed-feature space.[2] *Fixed-feature space* is created by immovable boundaries, such as the space within buildings. *Semifixed-feature space* refers to the space created by movable objects, such as furniture.

Fixed-feature space can provide important clues about the work environment or culture. For example, the physical location of an office may indicate the occupant's status or position within the company. The location and size of an office draw both visible and invisible lines around the worker. The walls or partitions of the fixed-feature space clearly define the employee's work space, while the employee's own sense of his or her place within that space provides further definition through invisible lines.

Within an office or work space, the arrangement of furniture defines the worker's personal space, and is a form of semifixed-feature space. For example, if a counselor chooses to sit directly across from a customer, the positioning of the chairs can indicate an adversarial, distant or competitive atmosphere. When possible, rearranging the chairs to be side-by-side or at angles to one another may create a more cooperative atmosphere. Instead of appearing at odds, the speakers appear to be working together.

Personal Space

In addition to the restrictions imposed by the environment, people act in accordance with the space restrictions they generate individually. *Personal space*, as described by Edward Hall in *The Hidden Dimension*, is the invisible bubble of space that surrounds each person.[3] People feel they "own" the air around them, and most of us know when that space is being invaded by another person. Some people become uncomfortable and guard their personal space carefully when this happens, while others welcome intrusion into their space and encourage touching.

The ways people use and misuse personal space provide nonverbal clues about society and about individuals. By manipulating personal space, people can bind a group together or separate themselves or their group from other groups. The amount of an individual's personal space depends on the culture and, in part, on the density of the population in which a person is raised. In some cultures, crowding is acceptable while in others people prefer to keep a greater distance between themselves and others.

Personal Space and Communication. In the United States people avoid sharing their personal space with strangers or even friends. People will move to the rear corners of an elevator and stare at the ceiling or floor numbers rather than look at or speak with their fellow passengers. If passengers accidently touch, they usually will mutter, "Excuse me," while moving as far away as possible. When meeting for the first time, people are sometimes uncertain about whether or not to shake hands. They may, in fact, step back to protect their personal space.

Any encroachment into an individual's personal space affects communication. When people value their personal space, they will attempt to defend that space. Most people back up or move forward when having a conversation in an attempt to find a comfortable distance. That distance varies depending not only on how well the participants know each other, but also according to the topic and tone of the discussion. While the invasion of personal space may inhibit communication, maintaining a larger distance can seem impersonal and thus can have the same effect. It is most effective to maintain a distance that is close but that does not violate a person's privacy. For example, when opening a deposit account, you might lean toward the customer, make eye contact and shake the customer's hand at the end of the transaction. In a business context, most people would not consider these movements as hostile invasions of personal space but as helpful gestures. If, however, you protected your personal space by leaning back and avoiding eye contact with the customer, you would make communication more difficult and quite possibly offend the customer. You may have protected your space by maintaining your distance, but lost the customer's goodwill in the process.

Personal Space Zones. Depending on whom you are speaking with and what you are discussing, the amount of personal space you need

Figure 4.1 Personal Space Zones

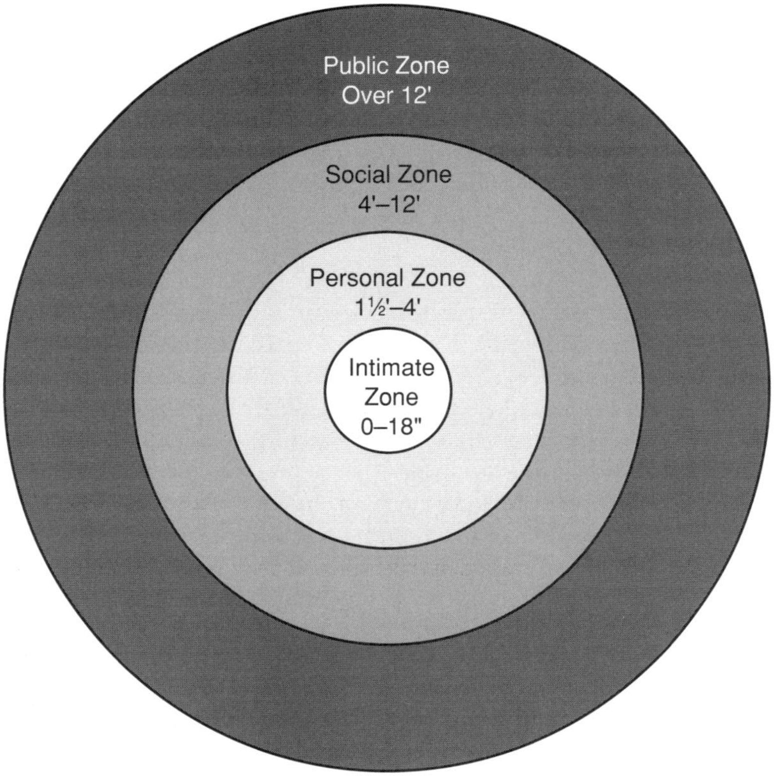

Source: Edward T. Hall, *Beyond Culture* (Garden City, N.Y.: Anchor Press, 1976).

to feel comfortable varies. The distance between sender and receiver that both find comfortable for communication is called a *personal space zone* (see Figure 4.1). This distance expands and contracts, depending on the relationship of the people, the type of discussion they are conducting, and other factors.[4] Personal space zones are identified as intimate, personal, social and public. Communication can take place in all these zones.

You may not always be conscious of where one zone ends and another begins, but you are always reacting to what you perceive as your personal space. As you move closer to or away from someone, you change your accessibility. Moving from someone's social zone into their personal zone may elicit a negative reaction that you should notice; if the response is positive or neutral, you will likely stay at that distance, or even move closer. Remember, however, that the ideas and limits of personal space vary among individuals, because of their personalities, backgrounds and culture. Respecting the personal space of others can help you maintain their goodwill, which in turn aids the communication process.

Intimate Zone. People generally feel that the intimate zone, a space between 0 to 18 inches around them, belongs to them for both comfort and security reasons. The only acceptable violation of that space is by relatives or friends. Thus, most people are comfortable when a friend or relative enters the intimate zone for close communication. If, however, someone who is not a friend or relative intrudes into this zone it may cause discomfort.

In business situations, most people are uncomfortable with close physical contact. They prefer to keep some distance between themselves and other people, retaining the intimate zone boundary. For example, if a co-worker steps forward to explain a procedure, a person may step back automatically to protect the intimate zone. The movement usually is not intended to be insulting but merely protective.

Personal Zone. For most people, the personal zone is a distance of one and one-half to four feet that allows casual conversation. At social gatherings, people will generally maintain this comfortable distance between themselves and others. The distance permits an exchange of sound, touch, smell, sight and other cues, without being too personal. Standing or sitting close to someone conveys friendliness and an interest in getting to know the other person. Still, a risk is involved that someone will perceive that his or her personal space has been violated. When this happens, it can hinder rather than enhance communication.

Social Zone. The social zone is usually a distance of between four and 12 feet, allowing you to interact with a stranger or an acquaintance without feeling threatened. Office reception areas and public furniture arrangements use the social zone to create space that both protects the speakers' personal space and yet allows communication. When the furniture arrangement does not suffice in protecting this space, people instinctively adjust. For example, the typical office desk may not allow enough distance between a receptionist and a visitor. To create more space, the receptionist may push away from the desk as the visitor approaches. This distance allows a pleasant greeting but protects the personal space of both the receptionist and the visitor.

Public Zone. A person's public zone extends beyond 12 feet, and is usually reserved for strangers and large groups of people. The public zone is the formal distance you place between yourself and a large group of people you are addressing. The further this distance, the more it discourages two-way conversation. When two-way communication is desirable, it is necessary to move closer to your listeners. For example, effective instructors will often move in closer within the public zone, even to the social zone, when they are seeking greater student involvement and feedback.

Kinesic Behavior

Body motion or *kinesic behavior* provides many nonverbal cues that can enhance communication. Like all nonverbal communication, kinesic behavior may be culturally based. *Kinesics* is the systematic study of the relationship between body motions and communication. Kinesic behavior generally includes movements of the whole body, gestures, posture, eye movements and facial expressions that enhance or detract from communication in some way.

Whole Body Movements

People often use various body movements to send nonverbal messages. Body movements send messages that indicate whether you are energetic or listless, interested or bored. Specific body movements can encourage an audience to join in the discussion. For example, during a presentation, a speaker might move into the audience to encourage greater involvement during the question and answer period. Or, a loan officer might lean back and relax during the loan interview so that the applicant also relaxes and contributes to the discussion.

At the same time you are giving nonverbal cues, you should also respond to the cues of your listeners. Their body movements provide valuable feedback that tells you whether to continue, repeat your point, go more slowly or speed up your discussion. If you are laboring through a long list of facts and you notice that people shift in their seats and look around the room, you should summarize the point you are making and move on. Their body cues indicate that they are uncomfortable—with your subject matter, your presentation or the environment.

Individual customers or co-workers also provide cues through their body movements. A customer who is shifting back and forth from one foot to another in a teller's line or nervously pacing while waiting to see a loan officer provide valuable nonverbal cues. You can relieve some of the discomfort by continually assessing nonverbal responses and by making adjustments as needed. By recognizing other peoples' nonverbal cues, you can respond appropriately to their confusion, hostility, boredom or anxiety.

Gestures

People often use gestures to accompany speech. A *gesture* is the spontaneous movement of the hands and body to express or emphasize an idea or emotion. Unlike whole body movements such as standing or walking, gestures refer to movements of only part of the body, such as the hands or head. Gestures can reinforce or contradict a verbal message and even substitute for a spoken message.

Although most people are unaware of their gestures, some speakers often make a conscious effort to accompany their speech with certain arm and body movements. Gestures vary from speaker to speaker and may vary even for a particular speaker. For example, if you are struggling with a frustrating problem with a group of co-workers, you might sigh, shake your head or throw down your pencil. But, if the problem was being discussed in a staff meeting, you might be more restrained in your gestures and only display a look of concern. It is important, therefore, to be aware of the context in which the gesture is made before interpreting exactly what the speaker meant by that gesture.

Restrained or inappropriate gestures also provide important cues about someone. Several studies have indicated that people attempt to hide lies by controlling their body movements. Their restrained gestures make it easy for others to detect that they are lying. Deceivers may look at the floor to avoid eye contact, wring their hands or stand perfectly still while speaking. Some people may even cover their mouths, almost as a cue that what they are saying is not to be believed.

Again, the circumstances surrounding the gestures must be understood if the individual gesture is to be interpreted correctly. Nervous gestures or habits do not always indicate dishonesty. A person who shifts nervously from one foot to the other while speaking may be uncomfortable or unsure of the statement rather than deceptive.

Eye Behavior

In addition to body movements and gestures, eye contact is often the primary means of nonverbal communication when people meet. More accurately than any other human communication signal, eye behavior reveals an individual's degree of interest in the person being communicated with and in the spoken message. For example, the greater your interest in the speaker and the topic, the greater your eye contact. Glancing away from the speaker can also help you in dealing with a large amount of information. Occasionally, glancing away may help you think about what was just said and how you may want to respond. As the speaker, you are likely to look someone in the eye when you have something important to say and you want the other person to listen carefully. Thus, eye contact can be used to maintain communication between people. However, it can also be used to end communication. For example, a discussion between a supervisor and employee can be ended quickly when the supervisor breaks eye contact—a clear signal that both the supervisor and the employee should move on to another activity.

Just as other physical movements reflect acceptable norms, so does the use of eye contact. Because eye contact is a primary nonverbal means of communicating, it is important to use it effectively. You can assess your effectiveness in using eye contact by observing others you consider to be effective communicators. Notice the intensity of their look and the way they use eye contact to send and receive messages. The intensity of a gaze often determines how a person reacts to a specific situation. If you greet a frightened, insecure customer with friendly eye contact along with a greeting, the customer is reassured of your involvement and interest.

If you have frequent customer contact, you have many opportunities to practice effective eye contact. During business discussions or transactions, it is important to keep the customer relaxed and open to suggestions. One way to control the situation and keep the discussion moving is to maintain eye contact with your customer. If you are uncomfortable looking directly into another person's eyes, you might try looking at an imaginary triangle on the person's forehead. By gazing at this area, you create a serious atmosphere and the other person senses that you mean business. Unless your eyes drop below the level of the receiver's eyes, you are able to maintain control of the communication.

Some people might attempt to block your gaze by blinking rapidly or looking around the room during a conversation. If this happens, you might need to try another approach to keep the lines of communication open. Use a visual aid, such as the person's account statement, to reinforce your discussion. You could use a pen to point to the area of the statement you are discussing to enhance your message and explain the situation. Then, lift the pen up to where your lines of vision would meet, which will encourage the customer to raise his or head so that your eyes can meet. By controlling the customer's eye behavior, you enhance the communication because the receiver hears and sees your message at the same time.

Facial Expressions

Although eye movement determines a great deal of overall facial expressions, the entire face must be considered in nonverbal communication. Research indicates that different emotions are more clearly represented in different parts of the face. For example, fear is easier to read in the

Reprinted by permission of UFS, Inc.

eyes than the mouth. People convey intentional and unintentional messages through their facial expressions. *Facial expressions* are movements of the face that reflect thoughts or attitudes, providing nonverbal feedback to others. The human face can produce hundreds of expressions over incredibly short periods of time. It may be difficult to interpret these messages correctly, however, because of the complexity of the human face. Because most people have learned to disguise their true feelings by controlling their facial expressions, their feelings may be hidden behind a well rehearsed smile or frown.

On the other hand, facial expressions can reveal a great deal and become the basis for a stranger's first impression. If a teller constantly frowns as customers approach his work area, he should not be surprised to learn that they think he is disagreeable. Although his supervisor may be pleased with his overall efficiency, his customers may find the facial expression unsettling. Customers expect tellers to be pleased to see them and happy to assist them with their financial concerns, but a frown indicates otherwise.

Our culture often limits strong verbal communication but permits nonverbal cues. Feelings that cannot be conveyed in words to a stranger because they would be too personal or too forward may be expressed subtly through your facial expressions. For example, although you cannot shout a friendly "Hello!" as each customer comes through your institution's door, you might smile as customers approach. This nonverbal welcome projects positive feelings. When peoples' facial expressions are friendly, communication is likely to be friendly and mutually beneficial.

Touching Behavior

Touch is one of the most effective ways of communicating nonverbally to other people. Although many studies confirm that people need physical contact to survive and to interact effectively, touching is often frowned upon in the workplace. Many people carefully guard their personal space and feel threatened by any physical intrusion. However, situations often arise that require tactile communication.

The most common touching behavior in the workplace is the handshake. Shaking hands is the modern form of an ancient greeting ritual. The empty right hand, which usually held a weapon, was extended toward the other party as a cue that neither party intended to attack. Over the years the handshake has been refined and changed in several countries. In most English-speaking countries, the palms are interlocked and the hands pumped three to seven times. The manner in which you extend your palm, apply pressure and shake another's hand communicates a great deal. Many people interpret a firm handshake to show honesty and strength and interpret a limp handshake to show insincerity and weakness.

In addition to shaking hands with customers and co-workers, some people may occasionally reinforce a verbal message through other forms of touch. For example, while praising a teller's work or attitude, a teller supervisor may pat the employee on the back. The intent and interpretation of the nonverbal message is particularly important in touching behavior since one employee may see the gesture as friendly while another sees it as an intrusion or, worse, as a sexual or physical assault. Especially in the workplace, use your judgment and refrain from any touching behavior that could be misinterpreted.

Paralanguage

Another element of nonverbal communication involves vocal cues that communicate various meanings. *Paralanguage* includes all vocal behavior other than the words chosen—how something is said rather than what is being said. The vocal effects that accompany the spoken words may also affect their meaning—complementing or contradicting the verbal message. The pitch (highness or lowness of tone), volume (loudness), rate (speed) and quality (tone) of your voice send nonverbal messages to the listener.

When you look directly into a customer's eyes and say, "I'm sorry about this error," you will complement the words if you speak in a medium-pitched, sincere tone. However, you would contradict your spoken words if you spoke brusquely while shuffling through some papers. In this instance, your words could convey a positive message, but your vocal behavior will leave a negative impression.

Vocal cues can influence a customer's response even more than verbal cues. In many cases, the customer will believe and react to the way you speak rather than your actual spoken words. Modulate your vocal pitch when you are in stressful situations, preventing your emotions from affecting your voice. Also, speaking at a slower pace will help you to sound more pleasant and agreeable, even when your information is unpleasant.

Artifacts

You can often gain important information about people from the way they adorn themselves or from the objects they choose to surround themselves with. These objects, or *artifacts*, like other nonverbal elements of communication, reveal people's attitudes and background. They can either enhance or detract from communication. Common artifacts include clothes, eyeglasses, jewelry, cologne and desktop displays, such as photographs or paperweights.

Artifacts usually are chosen with care to make a statement about the individual. Generally, people choose artifacts to enhance their features and to make themselves more attractive. For example, some people wear tortoise-shell eyeglasses for work to present a serious, conservative image. For evenings and weekends they may switch to brightly colored frames that create a more youthful or "fun" image.

People can use artifacts effectively to demonstrate a point. For example, removing your glasses when making an important statement often provides the other person with important nonverbal information. The removal of the glasses may be a nonverbal cue that tells the listener, "I'm about to tell you something important. If you weren't listening before, it would be a good idea to listen now." Further, it helps you establish eye contact, thus keeping the listener's attention and further reinforcing the importance of the message.

Artifacts may detract from communication as well. When a person wears too much cologne, it may be difficult to concentrate on the conversation. Instead, you may be thinking about ways to end the conversation because the environment is uncomfortable. Additionally, when a speaker frequently uses an artifact as a prop, the listener may concentrate more on the object than on the verbal message. The speaker who cleans his pipe every time he makes a point may be forcing people to concentrate on the gesture. Soon the listener is counting the number of times the pipe is cleaned rather than listening to the points being made.

Your selection of the many artifacts you use every day gives other cues about you. For example, you want to appear professional at your institution, so you might consider choosing artifacts that enhance that image. The savings institution business often projects an image of conservative safety to enhance customers' views of the business as a safe repository of savings and investments. For that reason, the artifacts you choose for work at your institution should project a conservative image. For example, clear eyeglasses might make customers feel more secure than heavily tinted ones.

The Communication Setting

Certain elements of a room or work space can enhance the communication that takes place there. Generally, the more comfortable you are in your work setting, the more comfortable others will feel and the more communication is enhanced. While you probably have little or no control over such features as office furniture, layout or the choice of carpeting, awareness of how certain features affect communication can allow you to adjust your work area to encourage effective communication.

The color scheme of your work area was probably chosen by an interior designer to project a certain image. Although you cannot paint the walls or change the furniture to suit your mood, you can personalize your area through subtle use of color. If your work area has touches of color that calm and comfort you, you will work and communicate better. You might also decorate the area with pictures, plants and other objects in an unobtrusive, businesslike manner.

Proper lighting can also create a more communicative atmosphere. People are more likely to listen and speak effectively when an area is adequately lit. Harsh lighting, however, may make people ill at ease. If you have control over the lighting in your area, you may find that a desk lamp, preferably incandescent, will encourage more sincere, relaxed communication.

Finally, temperature affects the quality of most communication. Most people are comfortable in the 68° to 75° range, and therefore can concentrate on conversation better when this range is maintained. If your work area has temperature extremes that you cannot control, you can try to minimize their effects by rearranging the furniture or by keeping warmer or cooler clothing on hand.

Time

Time and the emphasis placed on it are important elements of nonverbal communication. *Time* can be defined as the measurable period during which an action, process or condition exists or continues. In our society, people have many demands on their time. Families, careers and numerous activities and interests make time a scarce and valuable commodity. More than in previous times, people tend to live by strict schedules. For many people, the philosophy of time is simply "time is money." In addition, people tend to regard a certain length of time as appropriate for certain events. When the length of time for an activity extends beyond their expectations, then time can interfere with effective communication.

A person's attitude toward time results in nonverbal cues that affect the listener's understanding of the spoken message. When a customer is constantly interrupted during a business conversation by either the savings institution employee, telephone calls or other office personnel, the interruptions send the nonverbal message that the employee cares little about either the customer's schedule or what the customer has to say. Usually customers will feel resentful and demeaned by the experience. This insensitivity to the customer's time may even lose their business.

The value you place on time says a great deal about you. When you are consistently on time for meetings and appointments, you nonverbally communicate your respect for the time of others and your interest in the appointments. Arriving at work on time indicates respect for your responsibilities to your managers, co-workers and customers who depend on you.

SUMMARY

Communication is, at best, a difficult prospect if the participants cannot understand one another's verbal message. Differences in inflection, word choice or meaning can distort understanding and prevent effective communication. Communication is further complicated if the communicators are unable to understand the nonverbal cues that both speaker and listener are sending and receiving. Although we can control our verbal communication through careful word choice, nonverbal communication is seldom controllable.

Intentional or unintentional nonverbal cues aid or distort communication by providing information about the intended verbal message. We can learn to lie with words, but kinesic communication generally expresses our true intentions. Therefore, we tend to believe gestures and other kinesic behavior more than the verbal message.

To meet the challenges of communication, people must learn to give and receive verbal and nonverbal messages effectively. Every encounter with another person is a complex, challenging event. Each person provides a variety of verbal and nonverbal cues that contribute to the intended message. Correct interpretation of each person's word choice, tone of voice and kinesic movements leads to effective communication. Although culture and circumstance determine how verbal and nonverbal messages are sent and received, an awareness of those differences can aid communication. Your success as a businessperson depends on how well you communicate your intended message to others through effective verbal and nonverbal cues.

Chapter Questions

1. Explain the significance of nonverbal cues as they relate to human communication.
2. What is the science of proxemics? How does proxemics influence communication?
3. What is the difference between fixed-feature space and semi-fixed feature space?
4. Describe the four zones that separate people and affect communication.
5. Define *kinesic behavior* and give two examples of kinesic behavior that can aid communication.
6. What is paralanguage? Why is it important to effective communication?
7. Illustrate how the pitch, volume, rate and quality of a person's voice influence how the message is communicated.
8. Recommend at least two ways to improve communication through changing an environmental factor.
9. Explain how your understanding of the meaning of time influences your ability to communicate effectively.
10. Give three examples of nonverbal communication that complement a verbal message.

Footnotes

1. Ray L. Birdwhistell, *Kinesics and Context* (Philadelphia: University of Pennsylvania Press, 1970).
2. Edward T. Hall, *The Hidden Dimension* (Garden City, N.J.: Doubleday, 1966).
3. Hall, *The Hidden Dimension*.
4. Edward T. Hall, *The Silent Language* (Garden City, N.Y.: Doubleday, 1959), pp. 163–164.

References

Edward T. Hall, *Beyond Culture* (Garden City, N.Y.: Anchor Press, 1976).

Patricia Webbink, *The Power of the Eyes* (New York: Springer, 1986).

Albert Mehrabian, *Silent Messages* (Belmont, Calif.: Wadsworth, 1971).

© UPI/Bettmann Newsphotos

"A good listener is not only popular everywhere, but after a while he knows something."

Wilson Mizner
American dramatist (1876-1933)

5 Listening

Objectives

After reading this chapter, you should be able to:

- Define *listening*;
- Explain the role listening plays in communication;
- Explain two major uses of listening;
- Name three benefits that effective listening provides;
- List and describe four barriers to effective listening;
- Give examples of how those barriers can create communication problems in the workplace;
- Describe five techniques that can improve listening skills;
- Provide illustrations of how those techniques can be applied to communication in a savings institution setting.

COMMUNICATION IS A TWO-WAY STREET. It involves sending *and* receiving information; it requires both a speaker and a listener. Up to this point in the text, you have considered such vital communication ingredients as perception, effective use of words and nonverbal cues. However, skill in these areas cannot ensure effective communication without effective listening skills.

Listening skills are essential to communication in all settings. For years, psychotherapists, religious leaders and counselors have emphasized the importance of listening in all interpersonal relationships. Executives of major corporations have realized the effectiveness of listening skills in reducing costs, making effective use of time, building positive morale, increasing productivity, and developing good relationships within the organization and with customers.

This chapter explores the role that listening plays in your on-the-job and personal communications. It also examines some barriers that block listening and offers techniques that can help you overcome those barriers and become a more effective communicator.

LISTENING: A DYNAMIC PROCESS

Listening involves three separate but interrelated component processes: receiving sights and sounds, attending to them, and assigning meaning. All three processes occur at nearly the same time, and all three are necessary to listen.[1]

The first component, *receiving*, is the physiological process of hearing and seeing stimuli such as words, vocal cues and nonverbal cues. The second component, *attending*, refers to the process of selecting and then concentrating on certain stimuli. The third component, *assigning meaning*, involves interpreting or understanding the selected stimuli.

For example, imagine the following situation: On a particularly busy day, the computer system in your savings institution breaks down. One of the tellers looks up at the long line of impatient customers waiting while she processes each transaction by hand. The teller then turns to her supervisor nearby and says: "Look at that line! Do you think they'll manage to get the computers fixed before customers start walking out?"

The supervisor *receives* the message by noticing the teller's glance in his direction and hearing her words. He *attends to* the teller's words by giving his full attention to what she is communicating through words, facial expression, posture and tone of voice. He *assigns meaning* by analyzing, interpreting and understanding the message that the teller has sent: she is upset and wants assurance that something will be done about the computer problem.

Most messages in interpersonal communication have two components: the content of the message and the feeling or attitude underlying

this content. As the above example illustrates, both the content and the feeling are essential considerations when the listener assigns meaning to the message.

Uses of Listening

Hearing and listening are not the same thing. When you hear, you simply receive sounds: you can *hear* merely by being present. Listening, on the other hand, demands that you make sense of what you hear. To listen, you need to understand not only what was said, but what was *meant*. Listening requires attention and concentration. Effective listening serves two major uses. It enables you to receive and understand information, and it helps you build relationships with others.

Acquiring Information

The ability to receive and understand information is vital to success in every aspect of your life. Think about the various ways you use listening to acquire information. You listen as your supervisor or manager explains a new system of entering accounts. You find out about good films or restaurants as you chat with co-workers over lunch. As you listen to the new branch manager conduct a staff meeting, you discover her style of communication and management. Listening can also help you to classify, to organize or synthesize, and to solve problems.

Building Relationships

In addition to providing information, listening builds relationships and establishes *rapport*, a mutual trust between speaker and listener. In any interpersonal communication, some kind of relationship will develop between the parties involved. Through the use of empathy, a listener can help to ensure that the relationship is one of rapport.

Empathy is the ability to put yourself in the speaker's place and see the situation from his or her perspective—probably the most powerful and imaginative skill a listener can possess. Empathy is the basic ingredient in understanding others. When you empathize with others and see things through their eyes, your relationships with them will improve. By empathizing, you acknowledge their value as persons who are worthy of being heard, and they sense your respect for their feelings and opinions.

The Importance of Effective Listening

Of the four major areas of language development—listening, speaking, reading and writing—listening is the most basic. Listening is the first skill that we develop. Children learn to listen before they can speak, read or write. The ability to speak, read and write is dependent upon the ability to listen.

Adults also spend more time listening than speaking, reading or writing. A landmark 1926 study investigating the frequency with which adults use listening found that listening is the most often used form of verbal communication. The study revealed that adults spent 29.5% of their waking hours listening and 42.1% of their total verbal communication time listening.[2]

Benefits of Good Listening Skills

Listening occupies a large and important part of your life—from infancy through adulthood. When practiced effectively, listening skills can be the most valuable communication tools you possess. In your job, you spend a great deal of time listening to customers, co-workers, and supervisors or managers. Your ability to do this well translates into important benefits.

Positive Changes in the Speaker

Empathic listening is an important way to achieve positive changes in people's attitudes toward themselves and toward others. Researchers have found that people who have been listened to with sensitivity become more mature emotionally, less defensive, more democratic and less authoritarian.[3] Knowing that our thoughts and ideas are valued by others causes us to place a higher value on them and enables us to listen more openly to the thoughts and ideas of others.

Improved Communication

Skillful listening can also improve communication and group relationships—both in the personal sphere and in the workplace. People who have experienced a sensitive, empathic listener tend to listen to themselves more carefully and express their thoughts and feelings more clearly. In an atmosphere where empathic listening is practiced, individuals listen to each other more carefully, argue less, and incorporate other points of view more readily.[4]

Growth in the Listener

Listening also promotes personal growth in the listener. Not only does listening provide more information than any other activity, it also fosters understanding of others and self-awareness. When you put yourself in the other persons' places and listen empathically, your understanding of them increases as you begin to see why they feel and act as they do. And your self-awareness increases because, in the effort to understand others, you grow more sensitive to your own feelings and reactions.

Implications for Businesses

The positive effects of listening have important implications for businesses. Sensitive listening—with respect and understanding—is a first step in encouraging and developing employees' self-motivation. By listening to one another, co-workers can make individuals feel worthy of making contributions. Listening can result in a dynamic and productive organization.

Good listening skills are also invaluable tools for supervisors and managers. Experience and research indicate that the most successful managers and employees are those who have learned to listen well. Because they listen attentively and empathically, their colleagues and subordinates feel respected and valued. Because they listen analytically, they are able to solve problems and encourage discussion.[5]

The Cost of Poor Listening Habits

Despite the vast amount of time that adults devote to listening, and despite the proven value of good listening, most people are not good listeners. Research shows that most adults listen with only 25% to 50% efficiency.[6] In other words, most adults are not fully using their ability to understand and recall what they hear.

In our educational system, students spend up to 50% of their time listening, but that same system does little or nothing to teach students *how* to listen. Students who were not trained in listening skills are now employees who are untrained listeners, and inefficient listening in business is costly. In 1980, Lyman K. Steil, a professor of communications at the University of Minnesota, estimated that poor listening costs American business billions of dollars each year: "With more than 100 million workers in this country, a simple $10 mistake by each of them, as a result of poor listening, would add up to a cost of a billion dollars. And most people make numerous listening mistakes every week. Because of listening mistakes, letters have to be retyped, appointments rescheduled, shipments rerouted. Productivity is affected and profits suffer."[7]

In addition to measurable results, poor listening skills affect businesses in more subtle ways. Strained work relationships, low employee morale and bad customer relations often result directly from poor communication and listening skills between supervisors and employees, between co-workers, and between employees and customers.

Barriers to Effective Listening

If skillful listening can achieve such valuable benefits, and if poor listening habits are so costly, why are we not better listeners? Apart from a lack of training in listening skills, all of us encounter barriers that make good listening difficult and, at times, impossible. Four basic types of barriers are:

- physical barriers;
- physiological barriers;
- semantic barriers;
- psychological barriers.

Physical Barriers

Probably the easiest barriers to identify and overcome are those created by physical conditions, such as visual and aural distractions and distance. A setting with a high level of visual or noise disturbance hinders effective listening. Likewise, the greater the physical separation between speaker and listener, the greater the difficulty in listening effectively.

Often, the setting of a savings institution is not conducive to listening. The constant hum of heating or cooling systems, the clacking of teller terminals and typewriters, the steady droning of human voices, all create distractions that make listening difficult.

In addition, counters and partitions that physically separate tellers from customers and co-workers can obstruct interaction. Conversely, large open spaces in which simultaneous conversations are held at adjacent desks while people walk by on all sides can be equally damaging to effective listening.

Physiological Barriers

Physiological barriers to listening develop when the body's systems for receiving and reacting to sights and sounds do not function effectively. Physiological barriers include hearing deficiencies, inability to select or concentrate on stimuli, or the gap between one person's rate of speaking and another person's rate of thinking.

Hearing Deficiencies

One of the most detrimental barriers to listening—and one that may often be overlooked—is a hearing deficiency. As much as 10% of any adult group has some hearing difficulty. If a person suffers from a physical impairment that prevents hearing sounds at an adequate volume or that blocks certain auditory frequencies, his or her listening skills will be affected. Such hearing losses, if undiagnosed and untreated, will lead to continued frustration and annoyance in any attempts at communication.

Speech-Thought Gap

A second physiological listening barrier results from the difference between the rate one person can speak and the rate that another can think. People think at about 500 words per minute, while the normal speaking rate is about 140 words per minute.[8] Thus, you may have nearly 400 words of thinking time available to you each minute that you are listening. Because you can think so much faster than a speaker can speak, your attention drifts during the message. As you listen, your mind also attends to other stimuli.

At any one time, a number of stimuli in your immediate environment can compete with the message for your attention. These stimuli may be external, such as a customer's question, the blare of a fire engine, a message on the computer, or a co-worker at the next desk; or they may be internal, such as a distracting thought, feelings of pain from a sore tooth, or hunger pangs. When one of these stimuli interests you more than the message, you will stop concentrating on the message. For example, if you are hungry, you are probably more likely to listen to the teller at the next window describe the wonderful food served by the restaurant down the block than to the customer who is telling you about his problems with the automatic teller machine.

Semantic Barriers

Semantic problems can create a third barrier to effective listening. *Semantics* refers to meaning in language. When a speaker and listener have different understandings of the words being used, semantic barriers block communication between them.

One kind of semantic barrier can arise when the speaker and listener each ascribe a different meaning to the same word. Because of their unique experiences and backgrounds, different people give different meanings to the same words. For example, consider the difference in meaning that "liquidity" (taken out of context) might create in a discussion between a banker and a chemist, or the different images that the word "draft" would bring to the mind of a teller and a home heating specialist.

Another type of semantic barrier occurs when the speaker uses words that are unfamiliar to the listener. This communication problem can be particularly common among people who work in specialized fields that utilize jargon, such as the financial services business. Because savings institution employees frequently hear and use financial terms among themselves, they may be unaware of the confusion the terms create for customers or new employees.

For example, imagine the confusion of loan applicants who, during one interview, are barraged with new terms such as "amortization," "fixed rates," "ARMS," "escrow," "RESPA," "Truth-in-lending," "ECOA" or "pledged assets." Those loan applicants may experience

serious listening problems. Or consider the plight of the new teller at Secure Federal Savings who, in his first day on the job, is asked to look up a customer's PIN for the ATM and familiarize himself with telephone transfer MMDA and NOW accounts.

Psychological Barriers

Perhaps the greatest barriers to effective listening are those that stem from the listener's own feelings, concerns and attitudes. Such psychological barriers are common to nearly all communication situations. These barriers include:

- personal concerns;
- false assumptions;
- listener bias;
- negative emotional state;
- inattention.

Personal Concerns

When your personal concerns are more important to you than the speaker's message, it is difficult to be a good listener. For example, if you are expecting a telephone call about results of serious medical tests, you will have difficulty concentrating on your supervisor's explanation of a new data entry system. Nor will you be able to listen effectively to a worried co-worker when your thoughts are on an impending vacation. Barriers created by such personal concerns are understandable, but they make effective listening difficult.

In their book, *Egospeak*, the authors describe another listening barrier that stems from personal concerns: "The reason that no one listens, usually, is that our egos get in the way, in the sense that we're mentally formulating what *we're* going to say when the other person gets through speaking. Instead of digesting the other person's information, we are most often busy thinking only of how best we can *impress* him with our next statement."[9]

As an example, imagine that Sylvia, a clerk in the loan servicing department of a savings institution, approaches her supervisor with a suggestion for simplifying record-keeping. As Sylvia enthusiastically outlines her plan, Mitch, the supervisor, only half-listens. Mitch is thinking about improvement suggestions that *he* had made when he was a clerk. He decides to impress Sylvia by telling her about them. When Sylvia finishes describing her plan, she eagerly waits for Mitch's reaction. "Not bad," Mitch says. "That reminds me about how I turned around the whole payment system at this place. . . ."

Obviously, Mitch did not listen effectively to Sylvia. Perhaps not so obvious, however, is the effect such inattentive listening may have on Sylvia's future attitude toward Mitch and toward her job.

False Assumptions

A second major psychological barrier occurs when the listener falsely assumes that he or she knows what the speaker intends to convey. Often, instead of listening to what is actually said, people hear just what they expect to hear, and such "messages" frequently are not what the speaker intends. Savings institution employees who deal with similar kinds of transactions or persons throughout a day can be especially susceptible to this type of barrier.

For example, a teller who has heard repeated customer requests for cash disbursements in "tens and twenties" may automatically assume that her next customer wants tens and twenties, even though the customer specifically asks for "all small bills." Or a word processor whose supervisor asks that all letters be double-spaced may begin double-spacing a news bulletin when the supervisor has asked that it be single-spaced.

A statement made by George Bernard Shaw offers a word of warning and wisdom to this problem: "The only man I know who behaves sensibly is my tailor; he takes my measure anew each time he sees me, whilst all the rest go on with their old measurements, and expect me to fit them." Similarly, in our interactions with others, we can be effective listeners only when we approach each communication with renewed attention and receptivity.

Listener Bias

A third psychological roadblock to effective communication can be created by listeners' personal biases—either toward the speaker or toward the message conveyed by the speaker. Unfortunately, we occasionally judge the worth of others on the basis of such factors as the clothes they wear, the way they speak or what people have said about them. If we perceive these factors as negative, we may place less value on anything such people say and, consequently, fail to listen carefully to their messages.

A 1970 study illustrates the powerful influence that people's accents or speaking style can have on our impressions of them. In that study, personnel interviewers were asked to react to the placement potential of various individuals on the basis of voice tapes demonstrating the following dialects: general American white, general American black, light black, southern American white, and strong black. The interviewers (who were not told what dialects they were listening to) more frequently selected speakers with standard white dialect for upper-level managerial positions and speakers with the nonstandard dialects for lower-level positions.[10]

This bias could create serious communication barriers in a loan interview, for example, if a loan officer evaluates the applicants as "sloppy, poorly educated and probably irresponsible"—all on the basis of their dialect or the way they are dressed. The loan officer probably would disregard much of what the applicants say because the officer had already formed an opinion. In such a situation, it would be extremely difficult for the loan officer to listen effectively to the applicants.

Conversely, listeners may also form barriers if they feel that the speaker has power and authority. If the listener knows the speaker only as a "top-notch branch manager" or "a boss you'd better listen to," effective listening may be blocked by feelings of intimidation or by a sense of awe. Listeners may hear only what they would *expect* such people to say. Thus, listeners may be strongly influenced by a previous image and reputation.

We all tend to evaluate messages from our point of view, or frame of reference. It is usually easier to listen to an idea that is similar to our own view than to an opposing view. If the point of view expressed in the message differs from your own, your natural reaction may be to listen selectively—to listen for points to help you defend yourself or to support your own viewpoint. If the speaker is talking about a topic that you perceive as boring, you may label the message "not worth listening to." In such cases, effective listening will be blocked.

Negative Emotional State

The emotional state of the listener can, in itself, create a barrier to effective listening. Everyone has days of greater anxiety or irritability. Negative emotions such as fear, hostility and anger can cause listeners to close their minds to messages. Anxious or irritable people generally are not good listeners.

Negative emotions may also stem from more direct causes. At times, savings institution employees receive negative or even hostile expressions from irate customers or overworked supervisors, for example. Such encounters are always difficult, because they arouse negative emotions. The more involved you are in a particular situation or problem, the less likely you are to listen objectively to the feelings and attitudes of others. In general, negative emotions cripple intellectual powers and, consequently, listening skills.

Inattention

Finally, inattention to nonverbal cues can create barriers to effective listening or communication. As you discovered in the preceding chapter, nonverbal cues play a major role in communication. Listeners can miss the meaning of a message if they fail to notice the nonverbal cues that the speaker is sending. According to research, as much as 93% of a message's total meaning may be embodied in nonverbal cues such as gestures, smiles, eye movements and facial twitches.[11] Listeners need to observe such signals to comprehend the full message.

This type of barrier is quite common in on-the-job communication, where listeners are often occupied with several things at once. For example, a teller in a savings institution frequently receives customer questions or comments while he or she is operating a teller terminal or disbursing cash. Or a loan officer must listen to applicants' responses while filling out the loan application. Under these conditions, employees may miss nonverbal cues that accompany customers' messages.

Failure to observe nonverbal cues is unfortunate but often unavoidable. Other types of inattention that are even more damaging to communication, however, may be avoidable. For example, listeners who avoid eye contact, frequently glance at their watch, doodle, thoughtlessly interrupt or *allow* interruptions, will not only miss important nonverbal cues, but also signal a lack of interest in the speaker or the speaker's message.

Improving Listening Skills

While it is difficult to eliminate all of the obstacles that block effective listening, you can improve your skills at listening by practicing some of the following techniques:

- prepare your surroundings;
- take time to listen;
- build your listening vocabulary;
- assume a listening attitude;
- use good listening skills.

"I'm sorry, what were you saying? I must have dozed off for a second."

Prepare Your Surroundings

The ideal setting for listening is free from distractions and conducive to communication. Obviously, such a setting is not always available, especially during on-the-job communication. However, you can make even the most unlikely setting more conducive to communication.

In situations that require privacy or confidentiality—for example, discussing a customer's financial matters or correcting a subordinate—try to move the conversation to a secluded area such as a closed office or meeting room. If this move is impractical, you can create a sense of privacy by turning off a typewriter, putting down your pen and papers, stepping slightly away from other workers or customers, moving closer to the speaker, and responding in quiet, confidential tones. Such gestures help to create a shell of privacy and concern that encourages the speaker to communicate because you are giving full attention to the message.

Take Time to Listen

It often takes time to listen effectively, and good listeners must be willing and able to spend that time. Employees who never seem to have enough time can learn techniques to balance their time. You should be able to tell in the opening moments of an encounter with a customer or co-worker whether extra listening time will be necessary. If you decide that it will, you need to make a decision. Can you take the time right now to listen? Consider the other demands on your time. For example, how long may customers have to wait? If you do not have the time, explain the situation to the speaker and suggest a later meeting. However, in some situations, you may not be able to postpone listening. If, for example, an irate customer demands to be heard, you may decide that scheduling a later meeting is not wise. You can, however, consider referring the person to someone else in your institution who is qualified to handle the problem.

Build Your Listening Vocabulary

You can overcome some semantic barriers by increasing your vocabulary. Vocabulary size is an important variable in listening comprehension. You cannot listen effectively if you do not understand the words you hear. To improve your vocabulary, you can read widely, including newspapers, magazines, fiction and nonfiction books on a variety of topics; study vocabulary books; work crossword puzzles; take vocabulary building courses; and use a dictionary.

To improve your business or professional vocabulary, consider taking courses and reading books that deal with the savings institution business. You can also scan the business sections of daily newspapers and read the *Wall Street Journal*, *Savings Institutions*, *National Thrift News* and *American Banker* to keep up with the latest developments in the world of banking and finance.

If you frequently deal with customers for whom English is a second language (for example, Hispanic customers), you could enroll in a Spanish language class or find out if any co-workers speak Spanish and enlist their advice and their skills at translating.

Assume a Listening Attitude

A third strategy for improving your skills as a listener involves mental preparation. In order to be an effective listener, you need to make yourself ready and willing to hear what the speaker has to say. That is, you need to develop a listening attitude. Three suggestions can help you create an attitude conducive to effective listening:

- shift from speaker to listener;
- use empathy and objectivity;
- be positive.

Shift from Speaker to Listener

In any conversation, you must consciously shift from the role of speaker to that of listener. This shift can be triggered by sending a simple message to your brain, "Listen now." By making a conscious switch, it is easier to refrain from talking or interrupting the speaker.

Then you need to eliminate all the miscellaneous thoughts and distractions that constantly pass through your mind. All your attention should be directed at the speaker and to what is being said. You may also need to face the speaker, maintain eye contact and establish a personal space that is within a comfortable range.

Use Empathy and Objectivity

Two key ingredients in a listening attitude are empathy and objectivity. To practice empathy, you need to put yourself in the speaker's place and accept his or her point of view. This requires imagination and a willingness to accept differences between yourself and the speaker.

The willingness to accept another person's frame of reference also requires objectivity. That is, empathic listeners create a climate that is neither critical, evaluative nor judgmental. It is an atmosphere of equality and freedom, permissiveness and understanding, acceptance and warmth. Empathic listeners concentrate on understanding the message rather than critically judging it. In such an objective atmosphere, the speaker can feel safe enough to be open and honest, and the listener can begin to understand his or her point of view.

For example, imagine the following situation between two co-workers: Jeanette, the head teller who has worked at a savings institution for 30 years, strongly believes that customers and co-workers need to be addressed formally ("Mr." or "Mrs.") and wants her co-workers and customers to offer her the same respect. Brad, the new branch manager, advocates a more relaxed, first-name policy. Brad approaches Jeanette about introducing the new policy to the other tellers. As Brad begins to outline his ideas and explain his reasons for the new policy, Jeanette takes a deep breath and prepares to listen. Brad has always been friendly and respectful of Jeanette's skills, and she has learned to like him and respect his skills as a manager. And besides, she realizes, Brad *is* her supervisor.

Jeanette puts aside her own feelings and makes a real effort to understand Brad's point of view. As she listens, Jeanette gains a new respect for Brad. Even though she doesn't feel comfortable with the first-name business, Jeanette begins to see some advantages to his plan. Maybe the new policy can improve her relations with some of the younger tellers and co-workers, she decides. Thus, through empathy and objectivity, Jeanette was receptive to Brad's point of view and, by assuming this attitude, was able to understand and accept his point of view.

Be Positive

A final technique for establishing a listening attitude is to maintain a positive state of mind. As you discovered earlier in this chapter, negative emotions such as anger, hostility and fear can cripple listening skills. Conversely, positive emotions such as love, courage and compassion can increase a listener's openness to messages. If you care about the speaker, you will be more ready to see his or her point of view. Courage enables you to listen to views that may challenge or be critical of your own views. Compassion enables you to continue caring about the person who criticizes you.

In the illustration of Jeanette and Brad, for example, Jeanette's listening skills were enhanced by positive emotions: she realized that she *liked* Brad, and therefore she was more willing to listen to his point of view. She was courageous enough to see that the different approach he suggested might help her to improve some of her relationships at work.

Use Good Listening Techniques

A good listener is an active receiver. The listener must actively participate in the communication to gain the full meaning of the message. Here are some listening techniques to enhance your contribution to any communication:

- observe nonverbal cues;
- use the speech/thought gap;
- provide feedback;
- give good nonverbal cues.

Observe Nonverbal Cues

As noted earlier, a basic part of listening is observing. To be an effective listener, you must be aware of all the elements in a communication—both verbal and nonverbal—to receive the full meaning that the speaker is sending. You need to observe what speakers do with their bodies as they talk: notice how they stand, move, hold themselves, gesture and use their eyes.

Nonverbal cues are vital to comprehension. When any nonverbal behavior contradicts speech, the nonverbal behavior more likely determines the total impact of the message. Eye contact, postures, gestures, touches, distance, as well as facial and vocal expressions, can outweigh words and express the true feelings conveyed by a message.

For example, suppose a loan applicant says that she has had no problems with her credit rating. However, as the loan counselor questions her further, the loan applicant avoids eye contact, begins to sweat profusely, and seems short of breath. If the loan counselor is listening effectively, he will probably make a note on the application about the need for a careful credit check.

To be effective, listening requires careful concentration, keen observation, and conscious recognition of both the auditory *and* the visual aspects of the message.

Use the Speech/Thought Gap

Instead of being distracted by the gap in thinking and speaking time, you can use your thinking capacities to make yourself a better listener and enhance your understanding of the message. Instead of attending to stimuli that distract from the message, you can mentally review and summarize the speaker's words, anticipate his or her next point, note and assign meaning to nonverbal messages being presented, listen for what is *not* said, and identify the main idea of the entire message. These mental activities will help you avoid distractions by focusing all your energies on the speaker and the message.

You can also turn the speech/thought gap into a listening tool by using the extra time to make notes of the speaker's main points and to jot down any questions or reactions you might have to the message. Note taking can help you focus on the message and provide a reference for later action or review. However, in some confidential matters or personal conversations, note taking would not be appropriate and could block effective communication.

Provide Feedback

A third technique that can improve your listening is providing feedback. As you learned in Chapter 3, listeners use this technique to offer their understanding of the message to the speaker. Because understanding another person is more difficult than it may seem, it is important that listeners constantly test their ability to see the world in the way the speaker sees it. In addition, listeners must convey to the speaker that they *are* seeing things from the speaker's point of view. Two important ways to test your understanding of a message are questioning and paraphrasing.

Questioning. The ability to formulate simple questions is important in feedback. By periodically asking questions, you can enhance your reception of the message as well as alert the speaker to the need for clarification. If you do not understand something, whether it is a term, a direction, or a feeling, you must be willing to say so and ask for clarification.

At times, you may have to put aside your pride and discomfort in order to learn. As an illustration, consider the case of Lisa, who has recently been promoted to teller supervisor at First Federal Savings. Lisa is anxious to appear knowledgable and in control during her first days in the new position. When the branch manager explains the new, computerized passbook withdrawal procedures, she uses several computer terms that are unfamiliar to Lisa. Lisa wonders whether to interrupt the explanation to ask for clarification (thereby possibly appearing less competent to her supervisor) or to take the chance that one of the tellers can fill her in later. In this and similar situations, the listener must choose between maintaining an appearance of understanding the message or clearly understanding the message.

Effective listeners must also learn when and *how* to ask questions. At times, listeners interrupt someone to ask a question, only to discover that the question would have been answered later in the message. However, in complex explanations, where understanding later information depends on a thorough knowledge of earlier information, questions need to be asked and the material explained and clarified. Thus, Lisa may find that asking questions early will help her learn the procedure much more easily.

The best kind of questions, according to an expert in communication skills, are those that avoid implications in tone or wording of skepticism, challenge or hostility. Questions must clearly be motivated by curiosity about the speaker's view or by a genuine need for understanding.[12] You can seriously damage communication by using a condescending or angry tone or by asking a question that embarrasses the speaker.

Finally, when you do ask a question, you must be willing to listen to the answer—even if you disagree with it or if the answer takes much longer than you had hoped it would.

Paraphrasing. A second method of providing feedback is by paraphrasing, or restating the speaker's message in your own words. Like questioning, paraphrasing helps the listener clarify the message and alerts the speaker to any misunderstanding. Useful paraphrasing can be phrased in this manner: "If I understand you correctly, you're saying that . . ." or "In other words, you feel that . . ." Feedback not only helps to correct misunderstandings, it also tells the speaker: "This person is really trying to listen to me."

Skill in paraphrasing will develop if you work to listen to the message, restate the message in a simple, concise summary, and ask the speaker to evaluate the accuracy or helpfulness of your paraphrase. One technique can help you implement the technique of paraphrasing successfully: Each person in a communication situation can speak for himself or herself only *after* accurately restating the ideas and feelings of the previous speaker to that speaker's satisfaction. This may be a slow process, but you will find that it is an excellent method of improving your understanding—which is the goal of effective listening.

Give Good Nonverbal Cues

A final technique for effective, active listening involves the nonverbal cues that you, the listener, give. Speakers are affected by the nonverbal cues they observe in their listeners. Consequently, you will want to provide signals that indicate your interest and attention. Irritating nonverbal habits such as checking your watch, doodling, avoiding eye contact or shifting your feet can be replaced with actions that register interest and empathy. For example, to indicate that a customer has your full attention, you can turn away from distracting objects or people, look the customer in the eye, sit or stand in an alert position, nod your head occasionally, and use appropriate facial expressions to indicate your reactions to the message. Using such techniques conveys an attitude of interest and respect and encourages the speaker to continue talking.

SUMMARY

Listening skills are among the most valuable communication tools you can possess. Through effective listening, you can acquire new information and build healthy, productive relationships with others. Listening can also improve communication and effect positive changes in both the listener and in the person who is listened to.

Four basic roadblocks to effective listening are created by physical, physiological, semantic and psychological barriers. Physical barriers are the result of conditions such as visual and aural distractions or distance between speaker and listener. Physiological barriers—such as hearing deficiencies, an inability to select or concentrate on stimuli, or the speech-thought gap—can develop when the body's systems do not effectively respond to stimuli. When the speaker and listener do not share the same understanding of words that are being used, semantic barriers can block communication. Psychological barriers stem from the listener's own feelings, concerns and attitudes. Personal concerns, false assumptions, bias toward the speaker or message, a negative emotional state, and inattention can all create psychological barriers to listening.

A number of suggestions can help you overcome these barriers and become a more effective listener. You can remove or minimize distractions to make your surroundings more conducive to listening. By setting aside adequate time for listening or by referring the speaker to someone who *has* the time to listen, you can encourage good communication. Through such exercises as using the dictionary, reading widely, and studying books and periodicals that deal with the financial world, you can expand your vocabulary and thereby reduce semantic barriers to listening.

You can develop a good listening attitude by mentally shifting from speaker to listener, using empathy and objectivity, and approaching the communication with a positive state of mind. Finally, you can practice active listening techniques such as observing nonverbal cues in the speaker, using the speech-thought gap to mentally review and summarize the message, providing feedback through questioning and paraphrasing, and providing nonverbal cues that signal your interest and attention to the speaker.

Good listening skills can provide both personal and professional benefits. People who practice effective listening can improve their personal relationships and their professional skills and status. And savings institutions in which good listening skills are practiced will see greater profits, better time management, higher morale among employees and improved relationships with customers.

Chapter Questions

1. Name and briefly explain the three component processes involved in listening.
2. List the two major purposes of listening and give an example of how listening can accomplish each.
3. Explain what is meant by empathic listening and list three benefits that it can offer.
4. What are four basic types of barriers to effective listening? Give one example to illustrate each type.
5. How can the "speech-thought gap" block effective listening?
6. Describe a situation in which a semantic barrier might block effective listening in a savings institution setting.
7. What are two types of listener bias that can create barriers to communication? Give an illustration of each type.
8. List the five suggested techniques for improving listening skills and give a specific example of how a savings institution employee might implement *three* of those techniques on the job.
9. Why must an empathic listener try to be objective?
10. Briefly describe two types of feedback that are helpful in effective listening. How can such feedback help both the speaker and the listener communicate more effectively?

Footnotes

1. Andrew D. Wolvin and Carolyn Gwynn Coakley, *Listening* (Dubuque, Ia.: Wm. C. Brown, 1982), p. 50.

2. Wolvin and Coakley, p. 14.
3. Carl R. Rogers and Richard E. Farson, "Active Listening" (Chicago: Industrial Relations Center, The University of Chicago, 1957), p. 4.
4. Rogers and Farson, p. 4.
5. Allan A. Glatthorn and Herbert R. Adams, *Listening Your Way to Management Success* (Glenview, Ill.: Scott, Foresman, 1983), p. v.
6. Ralph G. Nichols and Leonard A. Stevens, *Are You Listening?* (New York: McGraw-Hill, 1957), pp. 5–6.
7. Lyman K. Steil, "Secrets of Being a Better Listener," *U.S. News and World Report* (May 26, 1980), p. 65.
8. Ralph G. Nichols, "Listening Is a 10-Part Skill," *Nation's Business* (July 1957), p. 4.
9. Edmond G. Addeo and Robert E. Burger, *Egospeak* (Radnor, Pa.: Chilton Book Company, 1973), p. xii.
10. Harvey L. Dubin, "Standard and Non-Standard Phonological Patterns as Related to Employability" (M.A. thesis, University of Maryland-College Park, 1970), p. 51; Larry Dobres and Cathy Gaffney, "Discriminative Listening Project" (University of Maryland-College Park, 1972).
11. Albert Mehrabian, "Communication Without Words," *Psychology Today* (September 1968), pp. 53–55.
12. S.I. Hayakawa, "How to Attend a Conference," *ETC* 3 (Autumn 1955), pp. 5–9.

Alfred Eisenstaedt, Life Magazine © Time Inc.

"Would you persuade, speak of interest, not of reason."

Benjamin Franklin
Poor Richard's Almanac *(1706-90)*

6 INTERPERSONAL INFLUENCE

OBJECTIVES

After reading this chapter, you should be able to:

- Define *interpersonal influence* and explain the role it plays in the workplace;
- Define *power* and identify the factors that determine who wields it;
- List and describe five types of power;
- Explain how power may be used efficiently and ethically in the workplace;
- List, define and describe the elements of persuasive communication;
- Illustrate how persuasion may be used efficiently and ethically;
- Distinguish among assertive, passive and aggressive behavior.

THROUGHOUT OUR LIVES we have opportunities to influence and be influenced by others. When we succeed in changing a person's point of view, we have used influence. When we change our view because of what someone has said, we have been influenced. Influence can be described as a process that involves "a change in one person's beliefs, attitudes, behaviors or emotions brought about by some other person or persons."[1] This chapter focuses on three types of influence—power, persuasion and assertiveness.

Influence in Work Relationships

Influence plays a role in the most familiar interpersonal situations. While we may think in terms of specific persuasive messages such as speeches or product advertisements, attempts to influence us occur in many other ways. Friends may try to influence us to vote for their candidate. A salesperson says we look great in a particular suit. The little girl next door sells us Girl Scout cookies. Not surprisingly, influence plays an equally important role in more formal social settings, such as the workplace. In the day-to-day operations of savings institutions, influence manifests itself in three types of interpersonal relationships—between employees and customers, between managers and employees, and among employees themselves.

Employee-Customer Relationships

Influence often plays a crucial part in the relationship between employees and customers. By offering information and advice, a financial counselor can influence the kinds of services a customer chooses. Financial counselors are not alone. Every savings institution employee—from the most junior teller to an institution's managing officer—can affect customers' behavior. Employee-customer influence may involve simple, straightforward actions. For example, a teller's warm and pleasant approach might persuade customers to encourage their friends to bank at that particular institution. Conversely, an attempt to influence customers may involve a complex series of actions by many people. An employee's influence on customers is reinforced by the institution's policies.

Manager-Employee Relationships

A second relationship where influence can be found occurs between managers and employees. The most common form of manager-employee influence is a supervisor asking a subordinate to learn a new task. Managers may also use influence to change subordinates' work attitudes and habits. For instance, a supervisor may encourage an employee to arrive on time, or a department head may persuade a supervisor to delegate more routine tasks. The supervisor usually attempts to influence an employee to conform to policies of the institution and, consequently, has the support of the institution. It may appear that employees have little control in these manager-employee relationships. However, as will be shown more fully later in this chapter, the way an employee responds to a manager's influence may change the manager's actions.

Employee-Employee Relationships

Finally, influence plays a part in the relationships among employees. All employees occasionally try to adjust the attitudes or behavior of their peers. Unlike the first two types of influence relationship, employee-employee influence is rarely, if ever, backed by institutional rules and regulations. In other words, employee-employee influence usually is informal, or not part of the structure of the institution, even though it occurs in a formal workplace setting. For example, one teller may try to persuade other tellers to organize their document drawers in a particular way. The savings institution may have no rules about where deposit and withdrawal slips should be kept. The first teller tries to influence the other tellers because he or she wants them to follow the system of organization he or she has adopted.

Power and Influence

Power is a necessary precondition of interpersonal influence. Power has been defined as a person's capacity or potential to influence others. However, the possession of power does not necessarily lead to influence. For example, teachers have the authority to influence their students, but not all teachers are able to influence their students' behavior. Conversely, an individual need not actually possess authority to have influence. That individual will exercise influence as long as other people think he or she has power. The perception of having power, then, is often as important as actually possessing it.

Power arises from the relationships among individuals, their needs, goals, desires and personalities. A person cannot have power outside of a relationship with another individual. According to one study, power arises in a relationship when one person depends on another.[2] A person might possess one or more resources that another person needs or wants, such as information, knowledge or social status; or a person may exhibit a tendency, such as showing disapproval or inflicting punishment, that another person wishes to avoid. In both instances, the first person has power over the second.

To illustrate this concept further, consider the relationship between John and Paula, two loan officers. While John may have some of the resources mentioned above, he will not be able to exert power over Paula unless Paula needs or wants the resources he controls. For example, if John knows the new procedure for screening loan requests, and Paula would like to learn this procedure, then Paula is dependent on John for that knowledge. The extent of Paula's dependency—and therefore the extent of John's power—hinges on the availability of alternatives to John's resources. If John is the only person who has this knowledge, then Paula will be heavily dependent on him. However, if other members of the loan department know the new procedure and are willing to share their knowledge with Paula, then she will not be very dependent on John.

Five Types of Power

The nature and extent of power among people differs from relationship to relationship. These differences create types of power that vary in the behaviors they influence. John French and Bertram Raven, two social psychologists, grouped these different types of power into five categories: reward, coercive, referent, expert and legitimate.[3]

Reward and Coercive Power

These two separate types of power often are grouped together because they are so closely related. *Reward power* exists when one person can provide others with something they want. For example, a supervisor uses reward power when she promises to recommend an employee for promotion if he quickly masters the procedure for opening savings accounts. In the workplace, rewards are not limited to promises of promotion. Rewards may be monetary—a pay raise or a year-end bonus, for example. They may be physical, such as a private office. Finally, they may be psychological, such as a word of praise on the completion of a tough task.

As illustrated in the adage of the carrot and the stick, reward power has its counterpart in coercive power. *Coercive power* is based on one person's ability to impose costs or penalties on others. These include disapproval, punishment or withholding rewards. A supervisor using coercive power might say, "I'll be very disappointed if you don't learn the procedures in two weeks," or "If you can't handle this, you won't be considered for a promotion."

Whether rewards or coercion will influence someone to change depends on three factors. In the case of an employee and a supervisor, the employee must believe that the supervisor can carry out the promises or threats. If, for example, the supervisor promised a promotion but the employee thinks the supervisor has no input into who gets promoted, the employee probably will not be influenced. However, if the supervisor's word weighs heavily in promotion decisions, the employee will comply more readily.

Second, the employee must feel that the reward or the threat matches the required change in behavior. If the supervisor offers a $50 bonus for learning the new procedure, the employee might feel that it is not enough for the effort required. Or, if the supervisor threatens not to recommend the employee for a promotion that the employee does not want, he or she may decide that learning the new procedure is too much bother.

Finally, the employee must feel that the requested change is appropriate. If the supervisor uses rewards or coercion to get the employee to cover for him for an hour every Tuesday and Thursday afternoon while he works out at the health club, she probably will feel that the request is inappropriate and she will refuse to comply.

Referent Power

The third type of power, *referent power*, is evident when an individual is viewed as a role model by others. Referent power can stand alone as a power base but serves as a very effective base when it is coupled with other types of power. Unlike other forms of power, referent power is often based on personal qualities of the individual, such as credibility, intelligence or, especially in the workplace, past performance. For example, subordinates may adopt the behavior and attitudes of a supervisor or manager who has risen rapidly through the organization.

Whatever the basis of referent power, its influence often is unintentional but strong. People are frequently unaware of their status as role models. In addition, identifying with another person is sometimes unconscious. The strength of referent power depends on how strongly a person identifies with a role model. When you admire the behaviors, beliefs and attitudes of someone else, you may be influenced by that person.

Expert Power

The fourth type of power, *expert power*, exists when one person possesses certain knowledge and skills that others do not have. Expert power is not based on a level of knowledge or degree of intelligence, but on that knowledge in relation to other's knowledge. Expert power has four important limitations:

- The strength of expert power depends on the level of knowledge or skill attributed to the expert.
- Expert power is limited to a person's area of expertise.
- Expert power is based on real power, not perceived power.
- Expert power can diminish when other people acquire skills in the expert's area of knowledge.

As an example, consider Dennis, the systems analyst of an institution's data processing department. He wields expert power over the other programmers because he developed the entire programming system, of which they know only part. The more the programmers perceive that Dennis's programming knowledge exceeds their own, the greater the influence of his expert power. The greatest threat to Dennis's influence is the acquisition of his specialized knowledge by the other programmers. As they learn his special knowledge and skills, Dennis's expert power will steadily diminish.

Legitimate Power

With *legitimate power*, the final type of power, one person can influence others because of the authority vested in him or her by the organization's norms and values. That is, you accept the influence of that person because you think he or she has the right to influence you and you have an obligation to comply. Supervisors and other managers have legitimate power because they occupy positions of authority in the organization and their job profiles state that they have the right to influence the behavior of their subordinates.

The strength of a person's legitimate power depends on the extent to which other people accept the norms and values of the organization. If people do not recognize the validity of the organizational structure, a person will have little legitimate power no matter what title he or she uses. In addition, this type of power is limited. The assistant manager of the loan department has legitimate power there, but not in the institution's other departments.

Overall, legitimate power can be extraordinarily influential, as indicated by Stanley Milgram's obedience experiments.[4] Milgram had subjects administer increasingly powerful electric shocks to "volunteers" who failed to learn fast enough. The subjects were told the experiment measured the effectiveness of pain in learning retention, but unknown to the subject, no shocks were delivered and the volunteers were merely acting. Most of the subjects administered all the shocks, even though the victims showed great distress and higher levels of shocks were described as extremely dangerous. When asked why they inflicted this "pain" on an innocent victim, most subjects replied that the experimenter—because of his position as a leading scientist at a prestigious university—had the authority to tell them to administer the shocks, and they had an obligation to recognize his authority and follow his orders.

Interaction of Types of Power

People rarely use these five types of power independently of one another. People with referent power, for example, may also use reward or coercive power, or a person with legitimate power may also be an expert in some field. Possession of one type of power may also enhance the effectiveness of another type. For example, people often accept that a person with legitimate power has the authority to exercise other kinds of power.

Reprinted by permission of UFS, Inc.

Responses to Power

As noted previously, power is the *potential* for influence. Power has to be *used* if influence is to occur. But what is the response of people when power is used to influence them? One study suggests that people respond in one of three ways: commitment, compliance or resistance.[5] The goal of using power to influence others is to gain their commitment—or, at least, their compliance—and to avoid their resistance. You can achieve this goal by understanding the effect of power.

Commitment

This response indicates that people accept not only the attempt at influence, but also the goals prompting that attempt. When those being influenced feel that the ultimate goals coincide with their own personal goals, there is no need for further use of power. The people being influenced have already espoused the same goals as the people with the power to influence. For example, data processors may learn a new computer program readily if they share the belief that it will make their jobs more interesting or easier, and they will not have to be told more than once to learn it.

Commitment often results when someone uses referent power, because those being influenced identify with that person's behavior, attitudes and beliefs. A person with expert power may also elicit commitment because those being influenced recognize the benefits of that person's superior knowledge.

Compliance

With compliance, people accept the attempt at influence and adjust behavior accordingly, but they do not accept the goals behind the attempt. In fact, they often have no understanding of these goals. For the most part, compliance results because people feel that the cost of complying is less than the cost of not complying. For example, if the manager of a loan department says to his or her loan officers, "I want your monthly reports on my desk by the end of the day, or you can come in over the weekend to complete them,'' most of the loan officers will comply. They may not know why they have to file monthly reports; they may even think the task is a waste of time, but losing a weekend is too great a price to pay for not complying.

Compliance may result from the use of any of the five kinds of power. However, reward power and coercive power are most likely to elicit this response.

Resistance

Not surprisingly, people often reject the influence others try to impose on them. People may actually be rejecting the request, the goals behind the influence, the person wielding the influence, or any combination of these. People may accept the request and even the goals, but resist the idea of another person attempting to control their behavior. Resistance most often arises when the person attempting to influence others generates resentment by abusing power. People rarely accept the influence of someone they dislike.

People often will mask their resistance with the appearance of compliance, but will undermine the request by taking more time than is necessary to complete a task, not finishing a task or deliberately making mistakes. They may also undermine the authority of the person attempting to influence them by complaining to their co-workers.

As an example, consider Larry, the assistant manager of the loan department at Riverton Federal Savings, who has been trying to get his employees to participate in a series of meetings he is leading after work to discuss improving department operations. Branch offices are represented as well as other departments in the institution. His attempts to influence his employees have not succeeded because he has misused his power consistently. He promised his employees overtime pay for attending the meetings, but when Larry's manager vetoed the overtime pay, Larry's credibility among the employees suffered. When reward power failed, he tried coercive power by telling people that absence would be a mark against them at their annual review. However, his employees knew Larry had little or no input in their annual reviews, so they continued to ignore the meetings.

In his frustration, Larry decided to come down hard on his employees. He gave people extra work, which they felt was unfair. He continually reminded people of his status as assistant manager, but this attempt at showing legitimate power alienated people further. When Larry threatened to monitor coffee breaks more closely if people refused to attend the meetings, some employees complied, but others began taking longer breaks than before.

Larry's attempts to use power met with resistance at each stage. As resentment against him increased, his ability to influence his employees collapsed. Ironically, in his efforts to make his department operate more smoothly, he actually made the situation worse.

Using Power Ethically

Probably the most important consideration for people who wield power is that they do so ethically. The relationship between those who wield power and those who are being influenced is naturally imbalanced, because the latter depend on the former in some way. It is therefore incumbent on those who wield power not to abuse this position.

Perhaps the best way to ensure that power is used effectively and ethically is for people involved to view power relationships as mutual dependencies in which all benefit from the relationship. For example, a manager can expect that an employee will "pitch in" and work extra hours if special circumstances warrant it. By the same token, the employee can expect equally fair treatment for time off for his or her own emergencies. In relationships characterized by mutual dependence, power advantages and imbalances are kept in check.

Persuasion and Influence

Like power, *persuasion*—attempting to alter the attitudes or behavior of others through verbal communication—is an integral part of interpersonal influence. Power and persuasion are closely related. For example, people who possess referent or legitimate power find that people are willing to listen to their attempts at persuasion. Furthermore, reward, coercive and expert power cannot be utilized without some form of communication.

Even though they are so closely related, power and persuasion are different. A person may possess power, even if he or she never attempts to influence others through its use. Persuasion, on the other hand, exists only when a person makes a direct, conscious attempt to influence the attitudes and behavior of others.

Attempts at persuasion may occur in relationships that involve as few as two people, such as a supervisor trying to influence the work habits of an employee. Persuasion may also involve large numbers of people, such as a department manager trying to convince his or her employees to accept some unpopular changes in policy. Regardless of the nature of the interpersonal situation, there are three primary elements in persuasion: speaker credibility, message persuasiveness and listener appeal.

Speaker Credibility

Most experts agree that the effectiveness of persuasion depends as much on the communicator as on what is being communicated. But what makes a speaker so persuasive that a listener will accept his or her message? A speaker's persuasiveness derives from his or her *credibility*,

Reprinted by permission of UFS, Inc.

or the ability of the speaker to inspire belief in listeners. Certain qualities combine to give a person credibility: expertise, trustworthiness and personality. Each of these traits must be perceived to exist in an individual to create credibility.

Expertise

When a speaker attempts to persuade, listeners ask themselves, "Does the speaker know what he or she is talking about?" To believe the speaker, listeners must feel that he or she is competent and knowledgeable on the issue. For example, your ability to provide accurate information and answer customers' questions on the features of various products enhances their view of your expertise and, therefore, your credibility. If you must ask a co-worker or your manager for the information a customer is seeking, your credibility is diminished.

Trustworthiness

Another question that listeners ask themselves is, "Can I trust the speaker?" This question tries to establish the speaker's intentions or motives for attempting to persuade. If the listeners believe that the speaker's intentions are good, honorable and ethical, they are more likely to find the speaker credible. However, if they think that the speaker has some ulterior motive—personal gain, for instance—they will think he or she lacks credibility.

Personality

Listeners also measure a speaker's credibility on the personal impression he or she creates. A speaker's physical attractiveness, enthusiasm or personal warmth may be a powerful source of credibility. At times, personality traits may be the sole measure of credibility, overshadowing expertise or trustworthiness as important factors. The use of film and sports stars in advertising illustrates this point. They may know nothing about the product they are advertising, and their motives are clearly for personal gain, yet their ability to persuade others to buy this product can be seen in the sales figures.

Message Strength

Without a message, how could a speaker persuade anyone to change their attitudes or beliefs? Because the speaker greatly influences the listener's perception of what is being communicated, it is difficult to ascertain the qualities of a persuasive message exactly. In general, a message's persuasiveness depends on the strength of its content and its presentation.

The Message Content

The content of successful persuasive messages frequently consists of an appeal to the listeners' reason or emotions, explaining why they should alter their attitudes or behavior. The reasons offered have to be believable and logical for the message to be persuasive. When explaining to employees why they have to learn a new computer operation, it is not enough for a supervisor to say, "Because I said so." It would be better to say, "Because it will increase our department's productivity," or "Because it will bring us into line with other departments." To be even more convincing, it would be useful to provide statistics and data that support the persuasive message. Finally, the reasons offered must be pertinent to the listeners. If a supervisor tries to influence his or her employees by saying, "It will help the other departments do their work," there will not be much response. The employees need to understand how that goal will affect their work.

The number and types of reasons a speaker needs to use in a persuasive message depends on the nature of the audience. Listeners who are not well informed on the issues usually can be persuaded by a few simple reasons. Well-informed listeners, on the other hand, may feel that a one-sided approach is a blatant attempt at manipulation by the speaker. These listeners respond better to hearing all sides of the argument. Messages should not be so simple as to insult the intelligence of an audience. These messages may result in a *boomerang effect*, causing the audience to react directly opposite from what the speaker intended.

Persuasive messages may also appeal to the listeners' emotions. Linking the content of a message to pleasant or unpleasant emotions heightens its effectiveness. For example, a personnel manager's efforts to limit smoking to certain areas of the building may succeed if he or she stresses the organization's concern for the rights of all employees, smokers and nonsmokers. Persuasive messages may also play on a negative emotion such as fear. The personnel manager may try to enforce smoking rules by conducting an antismoking campaign, informing people of the harmful medical effects of smoking. Inducing high levels of fear, however, may also result in a boomerang effect.

Finally, the speaker's presentation of the message may greatly affect the persuasiveness of that message. For example, listeners are more likely to be persuaded by a message delivered powerfully, moderately fast, with no hedging words and phrases like "umm," "ah," "okay" and "you see." In addition, nonverbal communication may make a message more persuasive. People seem to be persuaded by positive nonverbal behavior, such as smiles, eye contact or a relaxed, confident attitude.

Listener Appeal

To persuade effectively, you must always keep the listener in mind. Every listener has certain intellectual, educational, attitudinal and psychological qualities that affect his or her susceptibility to persuasion. Listeners who are less intellectually gifted, of a lower educational level or less well informed on the issues involved usually are persuaded more easily because they have less knowledge or experience to evaluate the speaker's message. A listener is more easily persuaded if he or she has little interest in the issues, and no investment in the subject. A listener's present attitudes or behavior also affects persuasion. A listener would be reluctant to adopt attitudes or behaviors completely opposite from those he or she holds. Finally, a listener's psychological needs may affect the readiness to be persuaded. A listener with a strong need for social approval, for example, may accept persuasion because compliance often results in approval such as recognition and praise.

Using Persuasion Effectively

To become more persuasive, you first need to scrutinize your communication skills. As noted earlier, credibility is the basis of a speaker's persuasiveness. You can increase your credibility, and thus your persuasiveness, by:

- gaining expertise and competence in areas you want to influence;
- clearly explaining your motives or intentions;
- emphasizing the personal qualities that make you more credible to others.

You can persuade others more effectively by considering the messages you communicate and the listeners to whom you communicate. By carefully studying a listener's intellectual, educational, attitudinal and psychological qualities, you can decide whether a message should be a rational or an emotional appeal and whether it should be one-sided or two-sided. Understanding your listener's needs and motives will increase the persuasiveness of your message.

As with power, the key to effective persuasion is ethical behavior. The use of unethical tactics such as lying, exaggeration and misrepresentation may aid persuasion initially, leading to what one writer calls "automatic influence."[6] These tactics take advantage of the propensity of an audience, when faced with a persuasive message, to comply without thoroughly reviewing all relevant information. In the long run, however, such unethical behavior is counterproductive.

Lying may help a speaker to persuade others once; however, the same group will question the speaker's credibility in later encounters. Exaggeration will have a similar long-term effect. Misrepresentation can take a number of different forms in attempts at persuasion. It can involve omitting facts or phrasing facts to make them sound attractive. For example, if a financial counselor said to a customer, "CDs are the single most popular financial instrument among our customers," but omitted the phrase, "whose assets exceed $20,000," the customer might choose a CD even though it is not in his best interest. Misrepresentation can also involve making people feel their behavior is inconsistent or unacceptable if they do not comply with an attempt at influence. For instance, a supervisor who asks a teller to work overtime because everyone else does misrepresented the job when she did not mention overtime requirements during the job interview. In the short run, misrepresentation may lead to automatic influence. Over time, however, listeners will question the credibility and trustworthiness of the speaker.

Assertiveness and Influence

People may possess an abundance of power and they may have a thorough understanding of the techniques of persuasion, but they still may not exert influence because they do not act assertively. Assertive behavior conveys to others that one is confident in the message that is being conveyed. This confidence adds to the believability of the message and increases its acceptability by the listener, thus enhancing the influence of the speaker. Being assertive, according to Arthur Lange and Patricia Jakubowski, means "standing up for personal rights and expressing thoughts, feelings and beliefs in direct, honest and appropriate ways which do not violate another person's rights."[7] In other words, assertiveness involves more than merely getting what you want. It also entails respect—for yourself and for the needs and rights of others.

Assertiveness is not a personality trait but a set of skills that can be used in interpersonal relationships. Being assertive involves both a mastery of and a willingness to use these skills. All too often, however, people fail to learn or refuse to employ these skills. Instead, people fall back on other forms of interpersonal behavior, such as aggression or passivity.

Aggression is often confused with assertiveness, since both behaviors involve standing up for your rights. However, the methods used in aggression ignore the needs and rights of other people. The goal of aggression is not mutual respect, but winning and domination.

Passivity, on the other hand, means not standing up for one's rights, or doing it in such a contrite or timid fashion that one's needs are easily ignored. Passive individuals submit easily to the demands of others, even when doing so is not in their best interests.

To show how aggression, passivity and assertiveness differ, it would be useful to examine how each operates in the same interpersonal situation. For example, Tom and Sandy are two tellers at a large savings institution. Tom has had some problems at home and he has been visiting a family counselor twice a week before work. He has not told anybody at work except his friend Sandy. Since Tom's counseling sessions frequently make him late for work, he has asked Sandy to cover for his tardiness. Sandy, however, does not think this is such a good idea.

If Sandy chose to respond aggressively to Tom's request, she might say, "Hey, why should I risk my neck for you? You've not exactly made a habit of going to bat for me when I'm in a bind. We've all got our problems, Tom, you're not so special. So look, pal, just forget it." It is easy to see how inappropriate Sandy's reaction is if she wishes to keep Tom as a friend and keep peace at the office. Her overreaction did not take Tom's needs into account and humiliated him for making his request.

In responding passively to Tom, Sandy might say, "Gee, Tom, that doesn't seem right to me. But, well, if that's what you want, okay. Sure, I'll cover for you." This passive response is also inappropriate because it ignores the needs and rights of both Sandy and Tom. Resentment on the part of both persons is the probable outcome.

In an assertive reply to Tom's request, Sandy might say, "Look, Tom, I understand that things are not going too well for you at present, and I really appreciate that these counseling sessions are important. But if I keep covering for you when you're late, eventually we're going to get caught. That means trouble for both of us, and trouble at work is the last thing you need right now. So, Tom, I just can't do what you ask. Why don't you explain the whole situation to the head teller? I'm certain she can find a way to accommodate you on the days you visit the counselor." By being assertive, Sandy rejects Tom's request forcefully, yet still recognizes Tom's needs and rights and deals with them respectfully and sympathetically. Sandy's assertiveness protects her rights and, at the same time, maintains a relationship of mutual respect between her and Tom.

Why People Choose Aggression or Passivity

Since assertiveness is such an effective form of interpersonal behavior, it would seem logical that all people would behave assertively. However, most people regularly choose aggression or passivity over assertiveness. What causes them to make such choices?

People often resort to aggressive behavior when they lack self-confidence or feel powerless. They may view others' behavior as intrusive or aggressive, or they may interpret situations as challenges or attacks. The only acceptable response for them is to strike out aggressively. Some people justify their aggressive behavior by saying such things as, "He provoked me" or "She insulted me in front of my co-workers." In their view, aggression is the only behavior that elicits a response from others.

Aggression may also result from past passivity. For instance, someone who has responded passively to a number of requests might explode in anger at the next request, or someone who acts passively at work may go home and act aggressively toward family members. Finally, aggression may result because people do not have the personal skills or self-esteem to employ other forms of behavior.

For most people, the initial outcome of aggressive behavior is positive. Aggression provides emotional relief, gives them a sense of power and gets them what they want. The long-term outcome, however, is often devastating. An aggressive person rarely has close personal relationships, frequently has problems at work and constantly fears retaliation from the recipients of his or her aggressive behavior.

On the other hand, people often behave passively because of their misconceptions about various types of behavior. For example, some people may choose to act passively because they feel it is polite or helpful. Other people may choose passivity because they confuse assertiveness with aggressiveness. Further, many people act passively because they feel they have no right to stand up for themselves or express their feelings. Some people may feel they have no right even to harbor certain feelings, especially negative ones, such as hurt, disappointment or anger.

Sometimes passivity results from anxiety about the outcome of assertiveness. For example, people fear that if they behave assertively they will appear selfish or other people will dislike them. Finally, people may opt for passivity because they have not mastered the skills required for other types of behavior.

The short-term and long-term effects of passivity are similar to those of aggression. Initially, passive behavior enables people to attain their major goal of avoiding conflict. Over time, however, passivity is destructive, since it can increase a person's resentment and anger, magnifying the loss of his or her self-esteem.

The Benefits of Assertiveness

Assertive behavior benefits people in their personal lives as well as their work lives. Most studies on assertiveness suggest that this form of behavior increases workers' effectiveness in five ways.

First, assertive people are more likely to achieve their goals. People are more likely to comply with statements that explicitly and concisely indicate what is required of them. Assertive behavior involves clearly stating rights, needs, ideas, opinions and goals. Further, people are more ready to cooperate with someone who recognizes that other people have rights, needs, ideas, opinions and goals.

A second way assertive behavior increases effectiveness at work is that it builds people's confidence, both in themselves and in others. People usually feel good about themselves when they act assertively because they handle situations forcefully yet reasonably. In addition, they feel confident that they can get other people to listen and respond to their ideas and opinions. When people feel confident in their own abilities, they usually are more willing to recognize the abilities of others.

Third, acting assertively requires people to take responsibility for their own behavior, rather than shifting responsibility to somebody else. When people feel responsible for controlling their behavior, their effectiveness increases because they are less likely to revert to passive or aggressive forms of behavior.

Fourth, assertiveness encourages people to take initiative. The control of behavior and greater confidence that results from assertiveness reduces people's fear of making mistakes or failing. Having overcome this fear, people are more willing to take the initiative in solving problems.

Lastly, acting assertively saves energy. Aggressive people use huge amounts of energy in fits of anger or in making plans to get back at those who they think have acted aggressively toward them. Passive people use an equal amount of energy worrying about making mistakes or doing something that will upset others. The energy that people save by being assertive can be applied to doing their jobs conscientiously and effectively.

Assertiveness: A Four-Step Process

Not every attempt at assertiveness will meet with success, nor will all the benefits mentioned above be accrued immediately. However, you can increase the effectiveness of your assertive behavior—and the likelihood of receiving benefits—by following a few simple rules. Malcolm Shaw suggests a four-step approach to more effective assertiveness: establish goals; do, rather than try; feel good about being assertive; and consider others.[8]

Establish Goals

Assertiveness involves getting what you want, but you have to know what you want before you can get it. You must decide exactly what you want to gain from assertiveness. If you want to be considered for the next promotion, let your manager know. If you are working long hours to complete your work and want help, ask for help. Once you have established your goals, keep them in mind as you apply assertive behavior.

Do, Rather Than Try

When people attempt a new or difficult task, they often tell themselves, "Well, I'll give this a shot." This statement allows for the acceptance of failure and, in part, invites failure. If, however, you tell yourself, "I'm going to do this," you establish a more positive view of your chances of success, and such a view will add to those chances. Therefore, when your goals have been established, say to yourself, "I will achieve these goals."

Feel Good About Being Assertive

In your attempt at assertiveness, put ideas of inadequacy behind you. Your rights, needs, ideas and opinions are worth standing up for, so stand up for them and feel good about it. Acknowledge to yourself that your views are just as important as the views of others. Tell yourself, "I'm important and so are my ideas."

Consider Others

A key to assertiveness is that it involves other people who have rights and needs. You must take other people—and their rights and needs—into consideration. For example, a co-worker's suggestions for improving a procedure may be entirely different from your own and you may even disagree strongly. However, it is important to consider them as important as your own. Comments such as "I think I see your point" or "That's an interesting suggestion" acknowledge that the views of another person are worth considering. Assuming such an attitude also increases the receptivity of others to your ideas. The key to assertiveness is, in essence, mutual respect among all those involved.

Summary

A major part of our everyday communication involves attempts at influencing other people. Being aware of the ways people have and use influence can benefit your savings institution in numerous ways—from smoother relations with the public and the business community to more efficient operations among internal departments. The savings institution is a people-oriented operation, and the more people know how to exercise influence with others in a constructive, ethical manner, the more effective they will be in helping make the business a success.

Chapter Questions

1. Name the five types of power and give an example of each.
2. What three factors determine whether reward or coercive power is effective?
3. Name the limitations of expert power.
4. In what three ways might people respond when power is used to influence them?
5. What is the best way for people to be certain they use their power in an ethical way?
6. What is the most important factor that determines a speaker's persuasiveness? What are the three components of this factor?
7. How can your credibility be affected by the power you possess?
8. How do you gear a persuasive message to a particular audience?
9. Is assertiveness the same as aggression? Name three reasons a person might choose to be aggressive rather than assertive.
10. What are the short- and long-term outcomes of passive behavior?
11. Name the five ways assertiveness can improve your effectiveness at work.

Footnotes

1. Bertram H. Raven and Jeffrey Z. Rubin, *Social Psychology*, 2nd ed. (New York: John Wiley & Sons, 1983), p. 402.
2. Richard M. Emerson, "Power-Dependence Relations," *American Sociological Review*, Vol. 27, No. 1 (February 1962), pp. 31–41.
3. John R.P. French, Jr., and Bertram Raven, "The Bases of Social Power," reprinted in Dorwin Cartwright and Alvin Zander, eds.,

Group Dynamics, 3rd ed. (New York: Harper & Row, 1968), pp. 259–270.

4. Stanley Milgram, *Obedience to Authority* (New York: Harper & Row, 1974).

5. Gary Yukl and Tom Tabor, "The Effective Use of Managerial Power," *Personnel*, Vol. 60, No. 2 (March-April 1983), pp. 37–44.

6. Robert B. Cialdini, "Principle of Automatic Influence," reprinted in Jacob Jacoby and C. Samuel Craig, eds., *Personal Selling: Theory, Research, and Practice* (Lexington, Mass.: Heath, 1984), pp. 1–27.

7. Arthur J. Lange and Patricia Jakubowski, "Assertive, Nonassertive, and Aggressive Behavior," reprinted in Abe Arkoff, ed., *Psychology and Personal Growth*, 2nd ed. (Boston: Allyn and Bacon, 1980), p. 161.

8. Malcolm E. Shaw, "Making Your Way Assertively," *Supervisory Management*, Vol. 26, No. 3 (March 1981), pp. 3–5.

© Don Minnick. Courtesy Life Picture Service

"No great advance has ever been made in science, politics or religion without controversy."

Lyman Beecher
American Presbyterian clergyman
(1775-1863)

7

Managing Conflict

Objectives

After reading this chapter, you should be able to:

- Define *conflict*;
- Compare the personal and organizational benefits of successfully resolving anger against the costs of not doing so;
- Identify at least four sources of conflict in the workplace;
- List the five typical responses to conflict and describe their optimal uses;
- Describe the steps involved in collaboration;
- Identify strategies for handling anger and other strong emotions;
- Apply communication concepts learned in other chapters to the challenge of conflict management.

SO FAR IN THIS BOOK, we have examined the dynamics of human communication and how knowledge of these dynamics can improve the way you work and interact with others. But even this knowledge cannot prevent problems and conflicts. *Conflict*, a prevalent feature of all human interaction, can be defined as disagreement about actions or viewpoints among people in relationships, groups and organizations. As described in earlier chapters, your unique personality is shaped by your perceptions, background, needs and values. When you seek to meet your needs or wants, you may come into conflict with other individuals or groups. You may even come into conflict with yourself when you have to choose one personal need over another. Conflict is a natural part of life, the logical result of being unique.

Communicating effectively in conflict situations is a major challenge in working effectively with your peers, subordinates, superiors and customers. A 1976 study conducted by the American Management Association concluded that managers feel they spend 24% of their time dealing with conflict, and that the ability to manage conflict is of increasing importance to success in business at all levels.[1] If almost one quarter of your time is spent coping with conflict, then learning how to identify and understand conflict situations and developing several ways to address and resolve them are crucial skills for both your personal success and the success of your institution. Perhaps it is best to begin by examining whether systems for handling complaints or conflict are in place and working. Researchers have found that, when conflict is repressed, it festers and grows. Are employees encouraged to work out their differences or keep quiet? Is customer feedback encouraged or resisted? What messages or policies regarding conflict are in effect in your institution? Constructive conflict management can help you to clear up misunderstandings, let go of old resentments, solve problems creatively, and work cooperatively and comfortably with others.

Communication During Conflict Is Difficult

As you already know, communication is a complex process, involving the value systems, emotions, thought processes and behavior patterns of both the sender of a message and the receiver. Conflict often arouses strong emotions in both the sender and the receiver, and these feelings influence communication, including the words chosen, nonverbal behavior, the participants' ability or willingness to listen to the message, and the filters present in interpreting the message. These strong emotions prevent people from reacting to conflict intelligently and constructively.

Conflict is neither a positive nor a negative situation, but rather an indicator of a disagreement or a problem that needs to be addressed.

However, people tend to focus on the negative elements and ignore the benefits. Our competitive American culture reinforces this reaction. People frequently view conflict in win/lose terms and respond by becoming combative or by withdrawing from the situation. These two responses, similar to the "fight or flight" reactions to stress described by researchers, are reflected by many common sayings, such as "Winning isn't everything, it's the only thing," and "If you can't say anything nice, don't say anything at all."[2]

People frequently respond to conflict situations with a combination of aggressive or defensive behaviors. For example, an angry customer visits a loan officer to discuss an error in the paperwork regarding a new home improvement loan. The customer aggressively voices his concern about the resulting costs, delays and confusion. His hostile behavior causes the loan officer to pull back and become defensive. In the ensuing argument, the customer's aggressive behavior includes some shouting, hostile judgments, finger-pointing, selective attention to what the loan officer is saying, and an unwavering belief that he is right. The loan officer, on the other hand, defends his position with folded arms, smugly mumbling a few qualifying remarks that show his unwillingness to admit any sort of error. Their emotions hamper their ability to communicate constructively, turning what should have been a simple problem into a heated debate.

Negative Effects of Conflict

Aggression and withdrawal inhibit people's ability to work together cooperatively and creatively. Aggression usually magnifies the conflict, spurring the receivers to become even more defensive of their views and more determined to "win" the struggle. Emotions may include anger or suspicion. Trust, willingness to cooperate, morale and job satisfaction decline. Energy is diverted from accomplishing work to coping with the conflict and its accompanying stresses. When people avoid a conflict, hoping to avert these negative outcomes, the problem usually does not go away. Instead, these negative outcomes occur because the problem behind the conflict was never clearly defined or resolved.

Benefits of Conflict

Conflict can be viewed positively, as an opportunity to identify, clarify and solve problems or resolve differences. You will read about a successful process for conflict resolution later in this chapter.

The benefits of this positive approach are many. Participants are more likely to solve problems because issues are clarified and explored openly and directly. Information and resources are shared, interaction and involvement is encouraged and finding solutions is easier. This process heightens morale and team spirit, and minimizes defensiveness.

Learning to handle conflict constructively will help you, your boss and your co-workers be productive, motivated and more comfortable on the job.

In addition to the benefits of a financial institution, good conflict management will improve the institution's relationship with its customers. A positive, understanding response to a complaint from a customer will not only retain that customer's loyalty, but can also build business. Satisfied customers may recommend your institution to friends. In addition, handling complaints will alert you to problems that might drive other customers away. When good conflict management skills are employed, you can learn from irate customers. By satisfying their concerns, you establish a positive service image.

Understanding Conflict

To manage conflict effectively, you first need to determine its underlying causes. While conflict is easy to recognize, it can be difficult to understand. Often the behavior in a conflict is only a symptom of other problems, sometimes unrelated to the immediate situation. The more that you understand about the causes of the conflict, the clearer you can communicate by targeting the appropriate problems to be discussed and resolved. Looking for patterns can reveal problems inherent in the institution and provide direction for a change in policy, procedure or structure. For example, if customers routinely misinterpret a form, perhaps the form should be changed. Tracking customer complaints as well as the types of conflict occurring among the institution's employees can provide information to use as a basis for identifying and solving problems. For example, suppose you gave your employees a new procedure to follow and later discovered that no one was following it. Before you become angry, discover the source of the conflict by asking yourself questions such as:

- "Did I make myself clear about what was expected?"
- "Did everyone have the appropriate training or skills for what was required?"
- "Did I explain why the new procedure was important?"
- "Does other unexpected work cause people to rush through the new procedures?"
- "Do we have any other areas of conflict that may be affecting this situation, or are people having conflicts with others at work?"

In this situation, the cause of the conflict could be rooted in any one of these areas. Determining the cause through good communication

skills—asking thoughtful questions to understand the issues, listening carefully, and then determining corrective action—will enable you to resolve this conflict. Hasty action, demanding compliance to procedures, scolding or accusing employees probably will not resolve the conflict.

Levels of Conflict

Three primary levels of conflict exist: intrapersonal, interpersonal and intergroup. But remember the dynamic nature of communication. Because our behavior affects others, it is possible for our action or inaction in resolving conflict on one level to change the situation and create conflict on another level.[3]

Intrapersonal Conflict

Intrapersonal conflict is conflict within yourself. It occurs when you want two different outcomes at the same time; when what you want differs from what you feel you *should* want or do; or when you believe in two conflicting ideas at the same time, a situation known as *cognitive dissonance*.

As an example of the first type, a part-time customer service representative has been asked to fill in for another customer service representative who is ill. However, she has planned a visit with her mother. She wants to please her boss and help the institution, but she also wants to visit her mother, since she has not seen her for several months. This situation creates intrapersonal conflict. An example of the second type of internal conflict occurs when a teller likes his job and wants to keep it but seeks a promotion because he feels he should be earning more money for his family. Cognitive dissonance can be seen in a worker who believes in respecting the boss's authority but also believes in challenging or questioning what he or she thinks is wrong. All of these conflicts are uncomfortable. As people express their discomfort with others, the turmoil present in intrapersonal conflict can result in interpersonal conflict.

Interpersonal Conflict

Interpersonal conflict occurs when two or more people differ with each other and struggle to obtain the outcome they want. Interpersonal conflict can occur at any level within an organization—peer to peer, boss to subordinate, or employee to customer. In the workplace, people often disagree over factual information, personal territory (who should be doing what) and agendas (goals and priorities). Certain causes of conflict occur more frequently between different parties. For example, peers tend to disagree over information, territory and agenda.[4] Conflicts between bosses and subordinates occur more about information and agenda and less about territory, while customer and employee conflicts occur most about information.

Intergroup Conflict

Intergroup conflict occurs when groups of people differ with other groups of people. These conflicts can be about information, agenda or territory. For example, bookkeeping and payroll may disagree about how certain data should be reported or processed, or staff may be in conflict with management about benefits and working conditions. The greater the number of people who are involved in a conflict, the more complex the issues become and the more careful and skilled the people need to be in their communication to bring about positive outcomes.

Sources of Conflict

Identifying the source of the conflict is key to both resolving the conflict and to preventing similar conflicts in the future. Your problem-solving efforts are only as successful as your understanding of the problem. In assessing conflicts consider the following:

- Who was involved?
- What led to the conflict?
- What actually happened?
- What are each party's feelings?
- How can the situation be resolved?
- What can be done to prevent similar conflicts in the future?

You can identify the issues at stake for yourself and others, recognize conflict patterns, examine the implication of these patterns to you and the organization, and formulate strategies or plans to resolve conflict more accurately. The many potential sources of conflict include value and perceptual differences, role pressures, personality differences, health and stress problems, and inaccurate or incomplete information.

Values

Because people are different, their value systems are different and provide a source of conflict. As discussed in Chapter 2, value is the importance or worth that people place on people, ideas or things. Value conflicts can occur on all three levels—intrapersonal, interpersonal or intergroup. For example, an assistant manager may feel an inner struggle about covering for her boss, whom she likes but who is missing work and making mistakes because of an alcohol problem. Individuals' beliefs and values frequently arouse strong emotions and are a common source of conflict. Resolving value conflicts while respecting an individual's right to believe as he or she chooses is difficult but important.

Perceptions

Perceptual conflicts resemble value conflicts. Frequently because of an individual's values or previous experiences, he or she perceives or sees situations differently from other people, applying different meanings or importance to the same situation. One supervisor may be eager to delegate to subordinates because she perceives benefits to all parties involved, while another supervisor perceives a suggestion to delegate as a threat to her territory.

Role Pressures

Each of us plays many roles on and off the job, and the pressures from these roles can cause many conflicts. Sometimes new supervisors have trouble being in a role of authority, and may bend rules for friends and former peers. In fulfilling their roles, different departments may have different and conflicting goals, as when data processing demands a procedure that other departments see as an unnecessary complication of their work. Conflicts between the demands of work and family are a common source of conflict today, as people feel the pressures of finding good child care, being available to children or aged parents, managing single-parent households, and so on. Work pressures can also cause us to be inattentive or irritable at home.

Personality Differences

Personality differences are another common source of conflict. Personality is an individual's personal identity or individuality. It includes an individual's total behavioral and emotional tendencies. Sometimes another person's personality is so different from yours that you may find it difficult to understand, work with or trust that person. Because you are more comfortable with people whom you perceive as similar to you, it may require deliberate effort to listen carefully to and respect others who are different. Sometimes conflicts over agenda are really personality conflicts, because each side cannot understand the other person's views or priorities.

Health and Stress

Health problems and stress make people vulnerable to conflict as they may have less patience or stamina in doing their jobs, poorer ability to absorb and process information accurately, and less tolerance for differences and demands. If you experience stress in your job, you may communicate less carefully than you might otherwise, which could have countless repercussions in interpersonal relationships, including how well people can work with you. This sequence may cause conflicts that lead to more stress and perpetuate the cycle.

Incomplete and Inaccurate Information

Incomplete and inaccurate information make cooperation at work extremely difficult, often creating conflict among individuals or groups. For example, information received via formal and informal channels may be at odds, leaving people confused about what to believe or how to respond. When an employee does not perform as expected, it may be because the supervisor has not given accurate or complete information, or the employee did not hear or correctly understand the instructions. When goals and duties are not clearly defined, co-workers may argue over territory or agenda. Customers may become upset when they do not understand a change in policy or procedure, or when new information about products or fees is unclear or confusing.

Typical Responses to Conflict

Understanding the levels and sources of conflict enables you to identify the issues that underlie unresolved conflicts. Likewise, understanding response options determines how you react to and resolve conflict. All people have a dominant pattern of responding to conflict that is learned and reinforced over time.[5] The organizational culture of your institution, especially the degree to which conflict is avoided or confronted, also affects your responses.

Frequently in conflict situations, people respond reflexively with their regular response style, unaware of options that might be more appropriate and beneficial. Some people have different styles in different settings. For example, they may be less or more assertive at work than in social situations, depending on their comfort with the people involved. Some people's response patterns are so strongly ingrained that they react the same way in every situation, whether appropriate or not.

Experts have identified five typical response patterns to conflict.[6] People either avoid conflict, give in or accommodate others, dominate or force their own way, seek compromises in which all parties get some of what they want, or collaborate with others to discover new solutions that meet the needs of all concerned. As summarized in Figure 7.1, each response option has advantages, disadvantages, preferred uses and

Figure 7.1 Five Basic Methods for Resolving Conflict

Methods	What Happens When Used	Appropriate to Use When	Inappropriate to Use When
Denial or Withdrawal	Person tries to solve problem by denying its existence. Results in win/lose.	Issue is relatively unimportant; timing is wrong; cooling off period is needed; short-term use.	Issue is important; when issue will not disappear, but build.
Suppression or Smoothing Over	Differences are played down; surface harmony exists. Results in win/lose in forms of resentment, defensiveness and possible sabotage if issue remains suppressed.	Same as above; also when preservation of relationship is more important at the moment.	Reluctance to deal with conflict leads to evasion of an important issue; when others are ready and willing to deal with issue.
Power or Dominance	One's authority, position, majority rule or a persuasive minority settles the conflict. Results in win/lose if the dominated party see no hope for self.	When power comes with position of authority; when this method has been agreed upon.	Losers have no way to express needs; could result in future disruptions.
Compromise or Negotiation	Each party gives up something in order to meet midway. Results in win/lose if "middle of the road" position ignores the real diversity of the issue.	Both parties have enough leeway to give; resources are limited; when win/lose stance is undesirable.	Original inflated position is unrealistic; solution is watered down to be effective; commitment is doubted by parties involved.
Collaboration	Abilities, values and expertise of all are recognized; each person's position is clear, but emphasis is on group solution. Results in win/win for all.	Time is available to complete the process; parties are commited and trained in use of process.	The conditions of time, abilities and commitment are not present.

Source: Lois B. Hart, *Learning from Conflict* (Reading, Mass.: Addison-Wesley, 1981) p. 149.

inappropriate uses. Communication is enhanced when the parties involved in a conflict understand the choices they have and deliberately adapt their responses to fit the situation.

Denial

Denial is the refusal to recognize the existence, validity or importance of an issue, often resulting in the refusal to discuss an issue. A person using denial is being both unassertive and uncooperative, resulting in an unresolved issue and unmet needs for both self and others. The goal of denial is to avoid conflict.

It is important to distinguish between denial as it is defined here and another closely associated concept. Sometimes people disagree with you about information or your view of reality. As a result, they may deny your wishes or requests. However, if they have acknowledged your views, then action in the form of communication can occur. Even though disagreement with or a refusal of a request is not the outcome you would like, it is preferred to a refusal to address an issue or to acknowledge it.

Denial manifests itself in several forms. When people withdraw from a conflict situation, they may change the subject, refuse to acknowledge that a conflict exists or appear indifferent. They may also postpone confronting the issue. For example, consider Joan and Leslie, two customer service reps who constantly denigrate each other's character and job performance in staff meetings. This situation creates tension for the entire group, interferes with the work of the meeting, and lowers morale. If their supervisor refuses to acknowledge that the conflict is a problem or dismisses the conflict by saying, "That's just Joan and Leslie," the supervisor would be responding with denial through withdrawal. Withdrawal also occurs when a supervisor tells the people in conflict to work it out for themselves. This may be appropriate if the supervisor knows that the parties have the skills to work it out, and if the supervisor has given clear expectations and guidelines regarding the resolution of the problem. Too frequently, however, the supervisor just abdicates responsibility because he or she is uncomfortable with the conflict and wishes to avoid it.

If the supervisor acknowledges that she should deal with this situation but continually puts it off, hoping the conflict will take care of itself, she is responding with denial through *postponement*. Postponement is an appropriate response to a conflict when the parties involved need a cooling-off period before they can deal with an issue, when the issue is unimportant or when more harm than good might come from addressing the issue. If postponement is chosen, however, a deadline for resolution should be set so that the problem is addressed eventually. Merely avoiding problems through postponement will only ensure that they continue and escalate.

When denial through withdrawal or postponement is overused, decisions may be made by default, without the input or participation of the parties concerned. Sometimes no decision is made. On the other hand, when people debate every problem, they may err in the other direction by not assessing when a conflict warrants attention. Some

measures to consider when deciding whether a situation deserves attention are the level of tension surrounding an issue, the necessity of a good flow of information to make sound decisions, and the flow of work accomplished.

Accommodation

Accommodation is yielding to or complying with the wishes of another person or group. When people place the needs and concerns of others above their own, they are accommodating. The goal of accommodation is to maintain harmony or please others, even when it means giving in on issues or smoothing over differences.

Two separate motivations can result in a decision to accommodate. The first is fear of negative consequences from conflict or disagreement. The compliant person decides to be unassertive in order to maintain harmony in the relationship. Perhaps you or someone you know has complied with a superior's decision that you disagreed with because you feared that challenging that decision would result in being fired or disciplined.

People who respond to conflict with accommodation frequently do so because they feel they have no choice. This strategy may lead to several unanticipated negative outcomes. First, communication tends to be one-sided, with the person doing the accommodating withholding comments about his or her feelings or thoughts about an issue. This prevents true sharing of ideas and concerns, and limits the quality and quantity of information needed for making decisions. Second, when people feel forced to accommodate, resentment and defensiveness build up, making future conflicts likely.

The second motivation to accommodation is anticipated gain, the expectation that cooperating with another will yield a positive outcome for the person who is accommodating. Sometimes people put another's interests first because it is emotionally gratifying. Accommodation can involve going along with an issue for anticipated political gain or goodwill, or for anticipated return of cooperation on an issue at a later time. Accommodation can be used during compromise, when a person gives in on one issue to get concessions on another issue.

Making a deliberate choice to accommodate can be a valuable strategic tool in dealing with conflict situations. Accommodation is effective and useful when an issue is of great importance to one party and genuinely unimportant to the other. For example, a customer may demand that account information be given to him in a certain format that is easier for him to understand. If this request complies with regulations, you may choose to do the extra work and accommodate the customer because you anticipate that the customer will appreciate you and your savings institution.

Accommodation can also be useful in a trade-off situation, that is, submitting to a request with the expectation that the other person will reciprocate. For example, a teller may agree to a supervisor's request for extra hours one week with the expectation that the supervisor will accept her request for reduced hours a few weeks later when her parents are visiting from out of town.

People who accommodate too often may feel that their ideas or requests are not receiving enough attention, or they may feel depressed or resentful when working with others. If they rarely accommodate others, on the other hand, they may notice that others are reluctant to share ideas and even accuse them of being unreasonable or inflexible.

Domination

Domination or force, when used as a conflict resolution strategy, involves the use of position, authority, influence or insistence to settle a conflict. When people use this style, they seek to meet their own needs and concerns at the expense of others. This is the most aggressive and least cooperative style.

Appropriate Uses

Domination is appropriate when a person is exercising legitimate authority which others recognize. Bosses, supervisors and board members direct work, assign tasks and make decisions as part of the responsibilities of their positions. At times, quick, decisive action is needed, as in a crisis situation such as a robbery or a flood in the computer room. At other times, difficult or unpopular stands must be taken to promote the goals of the institution.

Risks

People in authority sometimes overuse this approach. If a leader consistently imposes solutions or decisions, this approach may repress additional input or information. When people are dictated to, they become reluctant or afraid to volunteer ideas and depend on the supervisor for solutions. People frequently resent being excluded from the decision-making process. If overused, this approach can be damaging to an institution.

To gauge whether this style is overused, examine the morale of coworkers and subordinates, the level of support for decisions, and the amount of information or ideas volunteered.

Compromise

Compromise is the settling of conflicts or differences by mutual concessions. When people compromise they assert what they want and cooperate with others. A compromise solution meets some needs of each conflicting party. Some needs are surrendered or postponed for the sake of ending the conflict. For example, agreeing to a rotation schedule in which all staff share the peak work loads and the slower times is an example of a compromise solution. While fair and equitable, the solution may not meet the needs of all involved, nor may it be the best or only solution possible.

Appropriate Uses

Compromise is appropriate when the time available to solve a problem is short, when the issues are unimportant to either side or when goals are so divergent that collaboration would be impossible. At times, satisfying some needs and moving a process forward is the most desirable alternative. For example, consider a teller supervisor who is told by her manager to extend service during the holidays so that customers can transact business before and after work. Hiring additional tellers entails the time and expense of training, while the demands of working extra hours lowers morale and increases errors. The teller supervisor wants to improve customer relations, but not at the expense of the tellers. She can suggest a compromise in which service is extended an extra two hours a day but staff is reduced for those extra hours. The plan would call for two shifts of tellers, one shift working 8:00-4:00 and the other 10:00-6:00. In this compromise, the manager gains the extended hours, and the teller supervisor fulfills her duty without overextending her employees.

Inappropriate Uses

Compromise does have its drawbacks, however. When people forgo a goal for the sake of an expedient solution, they may resent the sacrifice and withhold support or commitment to the solution. If bargaining has not been done in good faith with mutual trust and honesty, one party may be manipulated by another. Sometimes the conflict reoccurs because the "quick fix" did not adequately address or uncover the underlying issues. For instance, in the above example the manager may not have informed the supervisor that the extended hours may need to continue through the next year, something that will need a more permanent solution.

Collaboration

Collaboration is a process of assertion in which parties cooperate with each other to understand each others' concerns, needs and goals, and to explore alternatives that address these concerns fully and to everyone's satisfaction. Of the conflict resolution strategies, collaboration demands the most effort, but it offers the fullest chance of a lasting solution to a problem. For this approach to be successful, the requirements include openness, candid and balanced communication, considerable communication skill, sufficient time to explore issues and options fully, trust, and commitment to finding solutions rather than winning or assigning blame.

Because this is the most demanding conflict management style, its use is not always appropriate. If a speedy decision is needed, if the parties involved are not committed to seeking mutually satisfying outcomes, or if trust or communication skills are lacking, one of the other options may be more appropriate. However, when each party can explore the issues completely, can seek an outcome that will meet its needs, and will support and implement solutions with commitment and enthusiasm, collaboration is the best method.

Applying the Responses to Conflict

As you have seen, each conflict resolution strategy has advantages and disadvantages. As a review, consider how each strategy could be applied to the example of the teller supervisor who needed to extend service hours and, at the same time, maintain high employee morale and productivity. With the avoidance option, the supervisor would not directly address the conflict and would continue to schedule the regular working hours. In accommodation, the supervisor would agree to the new schedule without proposing her idea. In domination, the manager may demand that the supervisor comply, imposing the new schedule on the tellers without regard for their concerns. Compromise might involve a rotating schedule in which all tellers shared the extra hours, with everyone getting some of the hours they wanted but not all. In collaboration, the employees and the supervisor would describe their scheduling needs and constraints to the manager, and propose solutions or options for addressing these while keeping in mind the staffing requirements for full coverage during peak traffic times. A flex-time schedule, such as one-week-early, one-week-late, might then be developed that meets the tellers' needs while also meeting the staffing needs of the institution.

How to Deal Successfully with Conflict

Whether using collaboration or compromise to resolve a conflict, several basic communication principles will promote cooperation, the acquisition of useful information and increased commitment to the outcome. Positive results are encouraged by defusing strong emotions through good listening skills, building rapport, communicating in clear and simple language, establishing a safe and comfortable environment, and engaging in a problem-solving process. These principles apply to both long-standing and short-lived conflicts between employees, supervisors and customers.

Defuse Strong Emotions

The first step in alleviating conflict is to defuse the intense emotions that accompany it. People frequently respond to conflict situations with a combination of heightened emotions, including fear, defensiveness and confusion. Sometimes people feel excitement, curiosity and hope as they look forward to working through issues. Strong emotions consume a great deal of energy and, as noted in previous chapters, can interfere with good communication. For example, if you resist the installation of ATMs at your institution, you might discount or reject important data about ATM usage because you are angry at the institution's method of introducing it. Defusing these strong emotions is the starting point for successful conflict resolution.

Good listening skills are key to calming emotionally intense interchanges. Asking for and listening to people's reactions to the conflict situation mollifies their feelings and provides information for understanding the issues involved. When people are allowed to express their emotions and are heard without arguments, rebuttals or other interruptions, they feel accepted. Even if the listener disagrees with what is said, debate is not appropriate here.

As you learned in Chapter 5, active listening involves skill and deliberate action. You can let others know that you are actively listening by repeating what you hear and using nonverbal confirmations such as head nods and eye contact. As you learned in Chapter 2, make sure your perceptions of the situation match the other person's. It is helpful to restate or summarize what has been said and to ask questions to clarify anything not understood. If the conflict is intense, listening becomes especially difficult. You may find yourself silently arguing with the speaker or jumping to conclusions about what he or she is thinking. Listening carefully to an irate customer who is yelling or making accusations can be especially challenging. Remember that customers want to solve their problem, not fight, and that solving the problem will be easier if you are attentive, calm and in control of the situation.

Build Rapport

By building rapport, you ease the communication process. In conflict situations, helping people to feel comfortable with each other also eases the tension of the conflict. One technique, paralanguage, is discussed in Chapter 4. Matching the way in which a person speaks or using his or her predominant communication channel (auditory, visual or kinesthetic) can create a sense of rapport and comfort between the parties involved. For example, if your customer repeatedly uses the words "frustrated" and "rip off" when complaining about a new service charge, your own use of the words "frustrated" and "rip off" when you discuss his concerns will help him feel understood and accepted. Mirroring nonverbal cues such as gestures, speaking rate and volume can also increase this comfort.

Use Clear and Simple Language

Good communication techniques include using clear, simple and direct language. This means using descriptive, objective language rather than judgmental language. It is a good idea when stating opinions and feelings to state directly, "I think . . ." or "I know . . ." instead of using more evasive language. Be sure that your verbal and nonverbal messages are congruent, not ambiguous or contradicting. These verbal techniques will provide the foundation for successful exchanges of concrete ideas and concise information.

Set Ground Rules

Ground rules help expedite conflict resolution because they establish some norms that people have agreed to follow. *Ground rules* are a set of assumptions about what is acceptable and how to work together cooperatively and comfortably to uncover issues and search for solutions.[7] Ground rules can concern how people treat each other, such as agreeing that each person has the right to be heard and that issues, not personalities, are the focus. It is important to establish the right to disagree, and to ensure the confidentiality of the discussion. These principles apply in all conflict situations.

Time and Location

Another category of ground rules concerns the logistics of meetings, including timing and location. All parties should feel ready—mentally, psychologically and physically—to invest energy in resolving conflicts. If one party is too emotional, has other pressing work to accomplish, or for any reason does not feel fully available, reschedule the collaboration effort, since premature scheduling can subvert the process. Schedule as soon as possible after the conflict has occurred and all parties feel ready, so that the issues are fresh and everyone shares the momentum of the conflict. Finding the balance between emotional readiness and timeliness requires honesty and thoughtful planning.

Scheduling adequate time for collaboration is also important, because full communication about complex issues and feelings takes time. More than one meeting may be necessary. A suitable location for the discussions is also essential. Neutral territory, such as a conference or meeting room, is often preferable to someone's office. Privacy and comfort are most desirable.

Who to Include

You must also decide who should be included in the problem-solving process. If the conflict is between two people, they may prefer to work alone or to include an arbitrator if they feel an impartial third party might facilitate the process. If two groups are in conflict, the meeting should include everyone or representatives from each group. All parties with a stake in defining or implementing the outcome should be included so that relevant information can be obtained. When the conflict involves a customer, involving others with expert knowledge of the issues or choosing to include the next level of authority is sometimes necessary to ensure that the customer receives the help he or she needs. Spelling out the ground rules before resolving a conflict can help people feel nonthreatened and positive about meaningful solutions. Once all the ground rules are established, conflict resolution can then begin.

Apply Problem-Solving Techniques

Resolving a conflict is solving a problem. Problem solving seeks the resolution of conflict through face-to-face confrontation with the conflicting parties. A problem-solving process includes the five steps described below.

Step 1: Define the Problem and Set Priorities

Defining the pertinent issues, both personal (such as behavior problems) and institutional (such as problems with policies or management practices), must be the starting point. If the relevant issues are not clear and agreed upon by the participants, it is difficult to resolve conflicts.

By focusing on needs and concerns rather than on goals or anticipated outcomes, you can avoid the tendency of becoming entrenched in a position. For example, when defining a problem with a customer, you might ask exploratory questions to sharpen your understanding of the situation. Questions can reveal concerns that the customer may not initially state or even have defined for himself or herself.

Separating facts from opinions, documenting facts and defining terms also assist the definition process. Once separate issues are identified, priorities among them can be set, thus setting a direction for problem solving. (Asking for a description of the desired outcome can be extremely helpful in determining a direction for problem solving.) Once participants understand all needs or concerns, they can explore multiple routes to satisfying them together. Once issues and concerns are identified, however, noting areas of agreement can decrease tensions and provide a basis for mutual problem solving.

Step 2: Brainstorm

Brainstorming involves creating as many possible solutions to the problem as can be imagined. It is important for people to resist the tendency to judge ideas during this process and instead generate ideas that may be impractical but may be useful in some way or may lead to a solution. In a conflict, this method can help solve the problem and enable the parties to work together. When working with a customer, ask him or her what potential solutions come to mind. Sometimes the customer may have thought of a solution that has not occurred to you and that may be simple to implement.

Step 3: Evaluate Possible Solutions

After the parties propose a number of solutions, they need to examine the pros and cons of each. A *force field analysis* can help to identify the resources or forces supporting implementation and those obstacles or forces resisting adoption of a certain solution. With a customer, you might write down the proposed solutions and then list the pros and cons of each.

Step 4: Choose the Best Solution and Take Action

After the solutions have been judged, you can then choose the best option. Next, develop action plans that specify who is doing what within the time constraints agreed to by the people involved. Interim steps or progress checkpoints should also be defined so that everyone is clear about the agreement and what to expect. Most importantly, document decisions so that everyone knows what they have agreed to. For example, you might send a letter confirming an agreement with a customer. This action provides a clear and concrete statement of the agreement and protects both the financial institution and the customer.

Step 5: Evaluate and Adjust

Once action is taken, it is important to evaluate on an ongoing basis the appropriateness and effectiveness of the solution. If the original plan requires changes, they should be considered a natural part of resolving the conflict rather than a sign of the solution's failure. Most good ideas and new efforts require some correction to their original plans.

Evaluation of the collaboration process as well as the outcome is important in assessing how people can work together smoothly in the future. Also, ongoing evaluation of conflict situations can reveal patterns and might enable you to minimize or prevent conflict in the future. Evaluation might reveal, for example, that two departments are not working smoothly together and could benefit from regular meetings. Self-evaluation might show that particular kinds of customers are difficult for you to handle. With this insight, you can resolve to be alert and patient during interactions with these customers.

Example of Conflict Resolution

Jane and Martha are two customer service representatives who are both interested in taking advantage of a new incentive program for selling CDs to customers. Both had sent out promotional material to their regular accounts as well as to a general institution mailing list. One day when Jane was not at work, one of Jane's customers came in and requested the CD. Martha served the customer, and in the process tallied up a sale towards the incentive bonus. When Jane returned, she was upset, feeling entitled to all or at least part of the bonus, since her efforts had brought the customer in for the sale.

To solve their conflict, Jane and Martha first listened to each other and acknowledged each other's feelings of anger and hurt (*defuse situation through active listening and acknowledgement of feelings*). They agreed a resolution was necessary, because they needed to know how to handle similar situations in the future, because they wanted to continue to work together comfortably, and because each wanted to receive the incentive (*define issues, stakes and goals*). They explained the situation to their supervisor and asked for time away from their desks and use of the conference room to work on resolving the conflict (*set ground rules and determine time and place*). The supervisor admitted that institutional policy was unclear, but since it was involved, she should probably be a party to resolving the conflict (*decide who to include in the problem-solving effort*). Everyone agreed and scheduled time to meet and resolve the issue.

In the meeting, they identified as common needs the ability to take advantage of the incentive program and to provide good customer service. Areas of disagreement included whether a customer could be identified as any one representative's customer and how to compensate each worker for her role in the sale (*define issues and desired outcomes*).

Brainstorming revealed many possible solutions, including splitting the bonus when more than one person participated in the sale, taking turns for full bonuses, referring customers to each other and requesting customers wait for their own customer service representative to serve them (*brainstorm possible solutions*). After considering these solutions, the group came up with a formula for rewarding shared sales with an amount for successfully soliciting the business and an amount for successfully closing the sale. In this way, each could contribute to her own success while helping the other and offering prompt service to customers (*choose, plan, document and implement the best solution*). Everyone felt satisfied. The supervisor agreed to write the decision in the form of a policy statement that was then approved by management and shared with remaining staff. Subsequent review indicated that the system worked well because all parties were rewarded for their efforts (*evaluate and adjust*).

Jane, Martha and their supervisor succeeded in solving this conflict because they followed the process, kept their focus on solving the problem, rather than fixing blame, acknowledged feelings, identified needs and concerns, and cooperated in exploring options. All of these activities relied upon effective communication.

Summary

Conflict management is an activity that involves all of your communication skills. Conflict arouses strong emotions in people, and for this reason many view it negatively. But conflict is inevitable between people with different goals and values, and it should not be viewed as necessarily good or bad. Rather, it should be seen as an opportunity to identify and solve problems and create a better working environment.

Conflict can occur between groups, between individuals or within a single person. Areas where conflicts often arise includes values, perceptions, role pressures, personalities, stress and health problems, and incomplete or inaccurate information. It is important to remember that in conflict resolution everyone has a right to express their own opinions and emotions.

Several typical responses to conflict have been identified. Denial and accommodation are two passive responses, compromise and collaboration are more assertive, and domination is aggressive. All these responses are appropriate and effective in certain situations, but collaboration offers the best chance for meaningful, lasting solutions to conflicts.

To resolve conflict successfully, you must create an atmosphere that reassures people and is conducive to communication and serious solutions. Emotions first need to be defused with a combination of good listening skills, rapport-building and direct talk. The ground rules for your problem-solving efforts should be established, including where and when to meet and who to include in the discussion. After this is done, effective conflict resolution can follow a problem-solving process that includes five steps: defining the problem; brainstorming solutions; evaluating possible solutions; implementing the best solution; and periodically evaluating the success of the solution and adjusting it accordingly.

Chapter Questions

1. How does good conflict management benefit a savings institution?
2. How can conflict situations interfere with good communication?
3. What communication skills are especially important during conflict situations?
4. Why must strong emotions be addressed before engaging in the problem-solving process?
5. How can policies or management practices contribute to conflict?
6. Name the five recognized conflict management options. What are the pros and cons of each option?
7. Identify typical conflicts between customers and employees in your institution. For each conflict, describe which conflict management option you would use and why.
8. Name three ways of establishing rapport with another person in a conflict situation.
9. Why must ground rules be set before beginning the process of conflict resolution?
10. Name the five steps involved in the problem-solving process of resolving conflict.

Footnotes

1. Kenneth W. Thomas and Warren H. Schmidt, "A Survey of Management Interests with Respect to Conflict," *Academy of Management Journal* (June 1976), pp. 315–318.
2. Lois B. Hart, *Learning from Conflict: A Handbook for Trainers and Group Leaders* (Boulder, Colo.: Leadership Dynamics, 1987), p. 7.
3. John W. Keltner, "Conflict," from *Elements of Interpersonal Communication* (Belmont, Calif.: Wadsworth, 1973), pp. 223–226.

4. Mary Jean Parson, "The Peer Conflict," *Supervisory Management* (May 1986), pp. 25–31. Reprinted from Mary Jean Parson, *An Executive's Coaching Handbook* (New York: Facts on File, Inc., 1986).

5. K.W. Thomas and R.H. Kilman, *Thomas-Kilman Conflict Mode Instrument* (New York: Xicom, 1974).

6. K.W. Thomas, "Conflict and Conflict Management," in M.D. Dunnette, *Handbook of Industrial and Organizational Psychology* (Chicago: Rand McNally, 1976); Martin Ross, "Coping with Conflict: The 1982 Annual for Facilitators, Trainers, and Consultants" (La Jolla, Calif.: University Associates, 1982), pp. 135–139; and Hart, *Learning from Conflict*, pp. 147–200.

7. Hart, *Learning from Conflict*, p. 165.

© Keystone Agency, Inc.

"How much finer things are in composition than alone."

Ralph Waldo Emerson
Journals *(1833)*

8 ORGANIZATIONAL COMMUNICATION

OBJECTIVES

After reading this chapter, you should be able to:

- Differentiate between an organization's internal and external communications;
- Define the terms *organization* and *organizational communication*;
- Name and illustrate three purposes of communication in a financial institution;
- Explain the effects of serial reproduction on communication and cite ways to control these effects;
- Compare and contrast communication flow through formal and informal channels;
- Identify communication that is supplied through organizational structure and climate, and cite ways that employees can use these channels productively.

COMMUNICATION IN A BUSINESS ORGANIZATION differs somewhat from communication in other settings. Just as you have one wardrobe for work and a different one for leisure, you need to communicate differently on the job than you do when you are at home or out with friends. Financial institution employees who recognize and take advantage of the differences between organizational and personal communication are more likely to succeed in their careers, fit in more comfortably in their institutions and accomplish more in their jobs because their communication styles at work are suited to a business setting and their institution's needs.

This chapter examines the nature of organizations and the purposes of business communication. It explains how information flows through a typical organization and how you can use a knowledge of communication sources and paths to give and receive the information you need. It demonstrates two general ways that people in business communicate: directly through organizational structure and indirectly through organizational culture. Throughout, you will see that effective communication in a business organization makes people's work life easier and more productive.

As you read, you can find answers to some questions that might seem puzzling or even irritating about communication at work. You will learn why, in many companies, all suggestions for improving service must go through an immediate supervisor before they reach the head of a department. Also described are the reasons that every individual in your institution needs to be able to communicate well. You will see how the informal "grapevine" of information can be both useful and harmful to an organization.

People use a different style of communication at work than at home because business communication takes place within an organization that exists for a definite purpose. To understand how you can communicate effectively in your institution, then, it is valuable to consider what makes a group of people an "organization."

The Purpose of Organizations

A business *organization* can be defined as a group of people who join together to accomplish one or more tasks based on joint needs and expectations. The group agrees on the tasks to complete and goals to set that will fulfill joint needs. To work together smoothly, the group also establishes rules and designates authority—who will do what and how work will be done.

Financial institutions are organizations whose goal is to provide financial services at a profit. For a number of reasons—historical, economic, regulatory—their financial services typically emphasize loans to individuals to purchase homes and other consumer goods. Profit results when the income from the loans is greater than the costs that the institution incurs from acquiring funds to loan out, attracting customers and meeting operating expenses. Profit enables the institution to stay in existence, pay salaries, serve community needs and in other ways reward people who work there. The focused purpose, work systems and cooperative effort add up to an organization.

Spring Lake Savings Bank illustrates how financial institutions fit the description of organizations given above. As you will see, effective communication is an intrinsic part of Spring Lake's business efforts. Twenty years ago, Spring Lake was a small institution with five full-time employees. All five employees knew each other well and worked side-by-side. Each person could help with co-workers' jobs so all employees communicated easily about their work and their common goals.

Today, after years of growth and a recent merger, Spring Lake Savings employs nearly 70 people full-time and has several branches in two communities. Some employees specialize in lending, others in deposit services, and others in finance, marketing and administration. In spite of these changes, however, each group member still depends on the efforts of all of the other employees in every part of the institution. So, if Spring Lake Savings is to continue to be successful or even to survive, all 70 employees must join together to accomplish tasks based on their joint needs and expectations, even though the group is much larger and more diverse. To work cooperatively and agree on needs, Spring Lake Savings employees must continue to communicate well with co-workers.

As you see, Spring Lake Savings, both in its earlier years and now, illustrates the characteristics of a business organization. Spring Lake Savings is a group of people who have joined together to accomplish work toward a specific set of agreed-on goals. Employees generally recognize that the institution's primary business goal, as with other businesses, is its survival. As in any organization, there is widespread understanding of how work is divided and the company's rules and lines of authority. Every staff member of Spring Lake Savings depends on others to keep the organization active and moving to accomplish its goals.

Communication Environments

Large or small, organizations need good communication to ensure that everyone works toward the same goals and agrees on tasks and rules. Otherwise, misunderstandings could slow the organization's progress or stop it entirely. In its operations, institutions depend on both internal and external communication.

Internal Communication

Internal communication takes place within an organization. You communicate with co-workers daily, and they communicate with you. These conversations may sometimes be casual and unstructured, but in fact good communication among employees helps to unify your institution's efforts to exist and prosper. It is important to remember that internal communication happens not simply because people in the work group feel friendly toward one another, but because people in any organization depend on one another to accomplish the goals of the group. Your willingness to accept and act on this point of view can make you a strong contributor to your organization's overall success.

External Communication

External communication links your institution to the outside world. One such link is between staff and customers. You and your co-workers must listen to and give messages to customers on a day-to-day basis. Your institution was founded to provide a special type of customer service, and customers' satisfaction with the quality of service they receive determines whether your institution will stay in business. In fact, many customers judge the quality of service on their contacts with staff, and they expect courtesy, reliability and responsiveness to their needs. Therefore, your communication behavior, both verbal and nonverbal, affects the success of your institution because it largely determines how customers perceive the quality of service.

Another type of important external communication occurs between your institution and regulators. Financial institutions must comply with constantly changing laws and regulations, and this compliance is communicated through verbal and written reports. Regulations also affect internal communication because your institution must communicate accurately how the laws affect people's duties and must develop ways for employees to learn these requirements thoroughly and promptly. In this area, your responsibilities include paying attention to news events, learning how your institution may be affected and, when necessary, adapting work processes to a change.

In both internal and external environments, the communication types and messages reflect the purpose of the business organization: to meet the shared needs of people in the organization as they work together for a common purpose. Thus the people who communicate, the way they communicate and the topics of the communication are all business-related to some degree.

Nature of Organizational Communication

Given the definition of organizations and a view of the environments in which they operate, it is easy to see how completely communication permeates the business day. Communication experts estimate that managers spend from 60% to 80% of every business day communicating.[1] In a customer-service business such as the financial service industry, communication occupies the majority of time for many other employees, too—especially tellers, retail banking staff, customer service representatives, loan officers and others who meet or talk with customers daily.

The definition of organizations also emphasizes the need for everyone to aim for shared goals and purposes. This is so significant that a familiar business axiom describes a CEO's most pressing assignment as "keeping everyone's nose pointed in the same direction." E. Linn Draper, chairman of Gulf States Utilities, recently said, "Even when managers agree on the big picture, it requires constant communication to implement policies."[2] In short, business organizations benefit when organizational communication is effective, and they suffer when it is not.

The Scope of Organizational Communication

It could be said that communication in business organizations includes all of the activities, events, procedures, and verbal or nonverbal expressions that anyone connected with the organization's mission observes or passes on to others. Therefore, *organizational communication* is a coordinated, purposeful exchange of information and feelings within a network of interdependent groups all directed toward the accomplishment of one or more major goals.

Recall the earlier description of organizations and see how communication fits in. If organizations consist of groups of people who work together to meet mutual needs, group members must be aware of the work that others do and what others need to learn from them. This exchange of information cannot occur without effective communication. The group must also communicate about task assignments and goals. Group rules and the agreed-on division of authority and responsibility must be clearly communicated and widely understood as well. If not, the efforts of the organization will be wasted.

Purposes of Organizational Communication

Organizational communication is a dynamic, on-going process, not a static result. Through the process of giving and getting messages, you and others in your institution receive the help you need to take action. And appropriate action is the overriding purpose of organizational communication. For instance, a customer's question leads a customer service representative to respond with help that results in a profitable sale. A memo on security procedures results in employee actions that protect the company's assets. Information exchanged during a department meeting draws attention to a procedural short-cut that saves time for everyone who uses it. If you look around you at any moment during your working day, you will see that you and everyone around you is communicating, verbally or nonverbally, and that people act on the messages they receive.

More specifically, communication in organizations, both internal and external, fulfills three major functions. Each function is vital to the effectiveness of the organization. The three functions are to:

- reach decisions;
- coordinate efforts;
- maintain the organization's well-being.

Reach Decisions

To be successful, a business organization needs to make good decisions. Good decisions, in turn, depend on reliable, relevant information. In most financial institutions, this information comes from many parts of the organization, including the board of directors, department heads, customers, informal committees and special task forces. Once decisions are reached, priorities and policies must be changed to reflect them, and the changes must be communicated throughout the organization.

Consider the following situation. The loan market in the communities served by Highland Federal has been soft. Because of this situation, Highland's senior management is looking for ways to cut costs without curtailing customer service. Since Highland recently added three ATMs, one option being considered is to cut back on lobby hours and reduce the number of part-time staff. A decision of the kind would affect many parts of the organization. Therefore, Highland's senior management decides to call a meeting to solicit information from a representative group of managers. Prior to this important meeting, an agenda with suggested "questions to be considered" was circulated to each invited staff member. All branches and departments were represented. By communicating with managers in the decision-making process, Highland can take advantage of their range of experience as well as draw information that department representatives have gathered from their staffs.

At the meeting, branch manager Denise Arch reports that one of her counselors said a major local manufacturer is expected to change from a weekly to a bimonthly pay period, which would significantly alter lobby traffic and transaction demand levels in her branch. Deposit services administrator Keith Warren reports on the success of a recent promotion to encourage use of direct deposit services that could reduce traffic on busy days. Sheila Kleine provides information on transaction activity on each of Highland's ATMs and Bill Harvey shares data that his staff has assembled on ATM breakdowns and repair costs. All of this information helps Highland's management reach a sound decision about lobby hours and staffing levels. Once the decision is made, most of Highland's employees can understand and support it because many of them had contributed information that was used in the decision-making process or had heard reports from their managers of the process Highland followed to reach a decision.

Of course, many decisions are made less formally than this. Suppose, for example, you were speaking with a friend during your lunch hour, and she gave you an idea on how to cross-sell your institution's line of credit service more effectively to current checking account customers by citing its ease, flexibility and low cost compared to the nuisance, cost and embarrassment of overdrawing an account. The next time a customer asks you to check a current balance or complains about an NSF charge, you might apply what you learned from your co-worker to help a customer make a decision. No formal directives or procedures were involved when you decided to try this sales approach, but you still acted with the interests of the organization in mind.

Coordinate Efforts

Good interpersonal communication is an effective way to coordinate individual efforts to reach the shared goals of the institution. People often possess information or knowledge that co-workers need. When they share this information openly, clearly and accurately, co-workers with different job duties and varied skills also may do their jobs better or accomplish more. When you help others by sharing job tips, passing along news, asking for clarification on a policy or teaching a correct job procedure to a co-worker, you use communication to coordinate with others to meet your institution's goals. By contrast, if someone withholds information that co-workers need—whether intentionally or accidentally—he or she creates a communication barrier that may damage the institution.

Consider the following example. On a recent Monday morning, Evelyn Jefferson's manager asked her to report to all branch managers that last month's payroll reports should be sent to the main office no later than Wednesday (a day earlier than usual). The reason for the requested change was that the accounting staff had just been asked to prepare several extra reports for the internal auditor and needed to get routine reports done early. Evelyn drafted a brief memo and put it into the interoffice mail about noon, but she forgot that mail for the Eastside and Green River branches was picked up only at 10:00 a.m. Mondays, Wednesdays and Fridays. The breakdown in communication from Evelyn's mistake caused problems for the two uninformed branch managers (who seemed to be uncooperative), for the accounting staff (who did not receive the full amount of help they needed) and for Evelyn's manager (who appeared to have given her poor instructions). If Evelyn had remembered that others were depending on information she had, she probably would have thought to phone the Eastside and Green River branches on Monday morning while communicating by interoffice mail with the other branches. This would have allowed all of the branch offices to coordinate their efforts in a timely way.

Maintain the Organization's Well-Being

Messages that keep an institution operating smoothly are known as *maintenance communications*. Some maintenance communication concentrates on tasks and getting work done properly. Other maintenance messages focus on the needs and concerns of the people who accomplish the work. Both types are critical to the health and continued success of a financial institution. A business cannot exist for long if tasks are ignored or improperly done. Equally important, a business needs motivated employees because people are more likely to consider the interests of the organization if they feel that their own needs are also being met. In these ways, effective maintenance communication provides stability and continuity to a financial institution.

Compliance with laws and regulations is a major type of maintenance communication in financial institutions. Every employee must know the laws and procedures that relate to his or her job duties. You may have received this type of information in procedural memos, tips from co-workers, formal training sessions or discussions with your supervisor. This knowledge protects the life of your institution. Preset work standards, department meetings and performance reviews are other examples of task maintenance communications that keep organizations operating effectively and ensure that people can do their jobs correctly.

The second goal of maintenance communication is to attract and retain qualified employees. Therefore, businesses tell prospective employees about benefit programs and arrange for staff members to receive information about salary changes regularly and confidentially. A company newsletter might list the names of new employees to help them get acquainted quickly and feel at home. The grapevine, described later in this chapter, can help to maintain the organization, too. Even customers' questions, compliments and complaints can help service staff learn how to satisfy the needs of the people who keep the company in existence.

Communication Flow

Consider the numerous ways you receive information at work—meetings, memos, conversations. All of these messages began somewhere, and many are sent through selected routes for particular reasons. The phrase "communication flow" is sometimes used to describe how messages move from one part of an organization to another. The word "flow" brings to mind an image of a placid river along which messages drift like autumn leaves until, by chance, they land somewhere on the grassy river bank.

The flow of messages in business organizations is seldom so peaceful although, at times, it is equally unpredictable. Sometimes, if you are lucky, the information you need comes to you directly and at just the right time. At other times, however, you may feel swamped with too much information or may think that a message from one source contradicts what you heard from another. There are even times when you need to search far and wide for vital information. A better understanding of the characteristics of communication flow can help you direct your messages to the right people at the right time. It can also help you receive and interpret messages from others more skillfully. One significant characteristic of communication flow is that most of it occurs through serial reproduction.

Serial Reproduction

Organizational messages start with one person and are directed to another. This results in serial reproduction. *Serial reproduction* simply means that each message is transmitted from one person to another person to another person, in a series. Each person serves as a link to the next by reproducing the message he or she receives and, at times, adding to it or reducing it when passing it on. For instance, the initial communication for a mortgage loan might be a phone inquiry from a customer to a receptionist. The customer's message might travel in a series past people in many different jobs: loan origination, appraisal, loan approval and loan closing. At every step of the way, the person who receives the message needs to get a clear and accurate message at exactly the right time. Each person should pass along information tailored to the next person's needs. As you probably have learned through experience, this does not always happen; instead, serial reproduction often involves problems.

Problems with Serial Reproduction

Problems in passing along clear, timely messages may arise at any point in the series. In the example of a loan inquiry cited above, the receptionist might write down the wrong phone number, the loan officer might fail to explain loan features fully to the applicant, a manager might misplace the notice of a meeting, an applicant might not supply all relevant credit information, and so forth. These types of problems during serial reproduction interfere with the smooth flow of communication that leads to the accomplishment of goals.

A further complication with serial reproduction is that, even when you try, it is almost impossible to pass along a message that is exactly like the original. As a child, you may have played a game called "Telephone" or "Gossip," in which everyone formed a line, began whispering a certain message at one end of the line, and waited to see how much the message changed by the time the last person heard it. Similarly, in the workplace as a business message is repeated from one person to another, the later messages are not exactly like the original. When playing a game, the garbled changes are amusing. In the workplace, they are at best a nuisance and at worst a serious problem. Business communicators, however, may head off the most damaging results if they are aware that messages they send or receive may undergo serial reproduction.

Researchers in business communication have identified a number of ways that serial reproduction tends to distort messages. Three general ways that are of special relevance to business people are leveling, sharpening and assimilating.

Leveling means that details tend to be omitted each time a message is repeated. This tendency is especially common early in the series. It also is more common when the message is complicated and long. Leveling is efficient because the message becomes shorter and simpler. The changes, however, may prevent the people farther along in the series from receiving the full amount of information they need.

Sharpening in serial reproduction means that as details are omitted, the remaining parts of the message seem more important than they did in the original. This can skew the message. As people relay the message, they also may supply unofficial extra information to try to fill any gaps they notice. As a result, the content of the original message may become even more obscured.

Assimilating means that each person in the series tends to notice and interpret the message from a unique perspective. Each person screens the message to watch for its most personal effects: "What does this mean to *me*?" This is a natural human tendency, but can be a serious flaw in organizational communication since success depends on everyone working toward shared goals.

Overcoming Problems in Serial Reproduction

Serial reproduction is inevitable in business communication and practically every other type of communication. Certain communication techniques, however, will help keep messages accurate and reduce distortion:

- Keep the number of links in your series as short as possible. Do not rely on others to deliver the message as you intend it. If many people need the same information, try to provide it through a meeting or an identically worded written message.
- Send a reasonable number of messages. By not barraging people with numerous messages, you acknowledge that their time is valuable,

and you increase the chances that they will have time to absorb your message.

- Present a manageable amount of information per message. People can only remember a limited number of details. If you limit the amount of information in any single message, receivers can focus more easily on your key points.

- Send complete messages. Include all essential information. A brief but complete message lowers the risk that leveling and sharpening will occur later in the series.

- Emphasize an important part of your message by repeating it, as in a summary, or by providing it in more than one medium. For example, follow up verbal communications with written memos. Or give a brochure with detailed information to supplement your verbal explanation of mortgage policies or savings options.

- Ask questions. If some parts of a message are not clear to you, check your perceptions by asking for clarification before you pass the message along.

- Be objective and fair. Listen for factual content and broad purposes rather than immediately reacting to the messages' implications for you personally.

- As a message sender, anticipate and address the concerns of your receivers; invite questions and encourage their feedback.

Serial reproduction helps explain what happens during the flow of communication, but not how links along the way are selected. How does one person in the series decide which other individuals should be given the message? One determining factor may be the organization's formal communication system.

Formal Direct Channels

Because business firms need communication to stay in existence, they spend a great deal of effort, time and money to ensure the flow of both internal and external messages. These efforts result in formal communication channels. Formal channels are intended to be systematic and efficient. They show employees authorized ways to move information routinely from someone who has it to everyone who needs it. Formal channels make communication a regular part of each employee's job duties rather than a special favor that people provide only for friends.

Organizations communicate in formal, direct ways through such means as scheduled meetings, written and spoken reports, memos and advertisements. You participate in formal communication when you

"I was just going to say 'Well, I don't make the rules.' But, of course, I do make the rules."

Drawing by Leo Cullum; © 1986 The New Yorker Magazine, Inc.

prepare a daily cash report, write down a phone message for a co-worker, attend a training session or meet with your supervisor for a performance review. Without formal channels, it would be impossible to reach decisions or coordinate efforts.

From the organization's point of view, formal communication channels have many advantages. They provide an efficient system to direct pertinent information to the person or group that needs it most. Quite often, formal communication happens at regularly scheduled intervals, such as daily reports, monthly meetings or annual events, so people can count on receiving information regularly. An added efficiency is that information spread through formal channels is controlled. By matching messages to the people or departments that need them, there is less informational clutter and overload. The board of directors does not need to know the daily cash reports of every teller window, because all the extra information would make it hard for them to focus on the "big picture" of how well the institution's financial plans are being met.

Good formal channels have the added advantage of equity. They are fair in that many people assume a share of the responsibility for spreading information to co-workers who need it. This system lightens workloads and still ensures that people have information they need to work together toward company goals. Moreover, formal channels distribute information impartially: everyone receives an identically worded message at a staff meeting or through written notices. Ideally, formal communication channels direct information from the people who generate it to the people who base decisions and activities on it.

Formal channels operate in three directions, which usually parallel the established lines of authority. Channels can flow downward, from management to staff; horizontally, between individuals or departments of roughly the same status; and upward, from staff to management. For example, a CEO might give a message of general interest to senior division managers. Each manager then communicates separately with department managers. These people, in turn, give the message to supervisors in their departments who communicate with their staffs and so forth. This is a downward path.

Horizontal channels move between individuals or departments of approximately equal levels in the organization. At Flintwood Federal, for instance, the deposit services staff regularly checks with loan origination to learn of local mortgage loan demands; branch administrative assistants get regular updates on loan rates from the central loan department to answer telephone inquiries and make referrals; and the data processing manager and marketing manager meet regularly on pricing services and managing a customer information file.

Still a third direction for formal communication in organizations is upward. For example, in Marshalltown Bank, upward communication occurs when the benefits coordinator in the human resources department compiles statistics on costs of medical insurance claims for the senior financial officer. Marshalltown's branch managers send budget projections to regional managers for review. And customer service representatives tally numbers on types of new accounts they open to give to their department head. All three channels—downward, horizontal and upward—ensure that information flows to others in an orderly way.

Unlike these simplified examples, information rarely moves along separate pathways. Even generating reports within a department can involve all three types of communication paths. Other factors also affect formal channels such as the decisions made by each level of manager about where to get data, which information is important, or whether certain reports or projections are incomplete and will need to be redone.

Informal Channels

A great deal of communication goes on outside the formal channels. A primary benefit of informal communication is that it adds a social aspect to the workday that would be absent if people worked in isolation. In addition, people working toward the same general goals can gain a feeling of being part of a team and recognize the contributions of the other players. Informal communication is of two general types: networks and the grapevine.

Networks

Networking in communication occurs when individuals purposely reach out to someone else with common interests, needs or affiliations. Networking is common in professional organizations. For example, people in a specialized work function, such as human resources or real estate appraisal, may join professional groups and attend meetings primarily to "network"—to get acquainted with other professionals with similar interests and to learn from the experiences of others.

In business organizations, too, people need the help of others and may form a network to keep in touch with those who can help them. Organizational networks are of two general types. In the first, the network is based on job roles or functions. A branch manager faced with an unusual customer request might pick up the phone and call another branch manager for suggestions on how to fill the need. If you ask a co-worker about her understanding of a new procedure that doesn't seem to be working right for you, the two of you have formed a network based on similar job duties.

A second type of network is more informal. Jason, Cherie and Jill are three tellers who carpool to work. Their conversations during the ride may touch on many subjects, but among them very likely will be some work-related talk. Marie and Betsy are customer service reps who work at adjacent desks. It is easy for them to talk every day and, as they become acquainted, to help each other out during busy periods. While they do not see each other away from the office as friends, at work they have formed a communication network.

Networks do not need to be extensive, permanent or established in writing. Instead, they tend to be functional and practical: they continue as long as they help the people in the network and they dissolve if one or several parties do not find them rewarding.

As a business communicator, you can make use of networking to help smooth out problems and gain skills. It takes initiative to create networks and, because they are voluntary, they must satisfy the needs of all members to continue to exist.

The Grapevine

The grapevine is a second informal method by which news and information travel from one part of the organization to another. It takes place through serial reproduction and can move downward, horizontally or upward through the company. In these ways it is like formal communication channels.

In many important ways, however, informal channels like the grapevine differ from formal channels. The grapevine has no structure, no formal rules and no legitimate authority. It is not orderly or equitable; news on the grapevine does not follow a schedule and it frequently bypasses some interested people while reaching others. Yet, informal channels exist in every organization. People often talk to one another casually about work. In casual conversation, news or speculations that are personally important or simply interesting spread from person to person.

Advantages of the Grapevine. The grapevine has acquired a bad reputation. Perhaps you have heard it said that the grapevine encourages gossip or wastes time. Since news you hear through the grapevine does not come from official sources, you may be skeptical about its accuracy. These opinions are widely shared.

However, informal communication channels have won support in certain ways. In some communication studies, the grapevine proved to transmit information more quickly than formal methods of communication. Moreover, under certain conditions, news reported through the grapevine can be quite accurate; some studies have found that the information is correct 80% to 90% of the time when it concerns non-controversial matters.[3] Since the organization benefits when news moves quickly and with considerable accuracy, the grapevine does have some advantages to the corporation.

Even so, business firms rarely plan for or encourage the grapevine. Why then does it thrive in nearly every business organization? The reason lies in the rewards it provides to individual employees who use it. Among its benefits are that the grapevine can:

- satisfy a need for social interaction among employees;
- give both senders and receivers of messages a sense of belonging;
- reduce anxiety caused by uncertainty, such as anticipation about how business problems will be handled or which types of changes are being considered;
- supplement or interpret news that was circulated through formal channels;
- provide a nonthreatening way for employees to discuss business issues of personal importance; and
- help management learn about employees' opinions or feelings without placing responsibility for unpopular views on a particular individual.

Problems with the Grapevine. In spite of its benefits, the grapevine still has many drawbacks as a means of communication. Because it is unregulated and unchecked, many of the problems of miscommunication mentioned so far in this book can arise. The consequences can reach far beyond the two individuals talking at any one time. Among the problems of communicating via the grapevine are:

- the credibility of information is questionable because it has no official source and no real method of verification;
- leveling, sharpening and assimilating are likely to occur;
- information may go through so many links that the resulting message bears little resemblance to the original message; and
- facts and opinions can become mixed as people interpret a message and retell it.

To examine the problems of grapevine communication, read the following dialogue that occurred during a coffee break and see how many of the above problems you can spot.

> ***Frieda:*** "Have I got news for you, Don. They've decided to close down the Westtown branch!"
>
> ***Don:*** "I wondered about all those closed-door meetings early this week. So I suppose they'll let all the Westtown people go. We sure don't need any more full-timers here at the main office."
>
> ***Frieda:*** "You know what did it, don't you? The Westtown branch manager and the assistant. I said from day one that they couldn't handle that assignment."

Don: "I sure hope our jobs are safe. So you think it was bad financial management? I can believe that. I took some loan documents over there one day for Jim and everyone was just kind of standing around, not doing a thing. We couldn't get away with that around here. How'd you find out, Frieda? I hadn't heard a thing."

Frieda: "You don't think they're going to tell us first, do you? I know a guy who dates the niece of a reporter at Westtown Press Publications. My friend didn't know the details but from his description it couldn't be any other place but us. But keep it quiet, okay? I've got to get back to work. See you later."

Don: "Okay. See you. Hey, Matt, come here. I just heard the Westtown branch is closing and our jobs are up for grabs. I don't know the numbers, but they had to be losing a bundle; everyone knows there was poor management there."

Both Frieda and Don were guilty of many communication mistakes, as they turned a small, unfounded rumor into a statement of "fact." They satisfied their own curiosity about the closed-door meetings, but in the process they jumped to conclusions based on an outside source and even sullied the reputation of two fellow employees. Frieda didn't question the unofficial nature of her source of information and placed the blame on the branch manager and the assistant, whom she apparently was predisposed to dislike. Don's insecurity about his own job, his poor listening skills and his eagerness to pass along and expand the rumor fueled the speculation further.

Overcoming the Problems of the Grapevine. As the example of Don and Frieda shows, informal communication can cause major problems for an organization in a short period of time. To avoid these problems, remember what previous chapters have said about listening carefully and separating fact from opinion.

Try to do the following when you take part in informal communication in your institution:

- Consider the credibility of your source. If the source is questionable, don't pass the message along.
- Differentiate between facts and opinions. If you pass along opinions, identify them as such and name your source.
- Paraphrase or restate unclear messages and check with the speaker to see if your interpretation of what was said is correct.
- Resist adding to the original message.
- Avoid the processes of leveling, sharpening and assimilating. If your source is credible, pass on the message as it was given to you.

No business organization can exist without formal and informal channels of communication. To remain a viable entity, an organization must try to take advantage of both types to convey its organizational goals to employees.

Communicating Organizational Goals

Organizations need to be sure that all group members know about and agree on goals. Similarly, institutions need to communicate about tasks in a timely and efficient way, and establish a work environment that clarifies expectations and motivates everyone to accomplish both broad and specific goals. Institutions try to accomplish all of this through two distinct elements of organizational life: structure and culture.

Structure

Generally, *structure* is the arrangement or configuration of an entity's interrelated parts or elements. The structure of a house includes floors and walls, plumbing and electrical connections, ducts for heating or cooling, and so forth. The various elements serve different functions but they all are needed to complete the structure of the house. In a business organization, these working elements are job specialties, departments, work procedures, policies and the like.

When you started to work for your institution, its structure probably was not clear to you. You probably began to get a sense of the structure by learning your own job and those of your peers, and gradually expanded your knowledge to include the work and staff of other departments and different service specialties. With each new piece of information about structure, you became a better communicator in your institution. You had a better understanding of where to get information, explanations or approvals. This helped you accomplish your own tasks. You also learned which information co-workers needed from you in order to do their work well. Today, your increasingly broad and accurate knowledge of structure improves the customer service you provide and strengthens your company.

Each institution has its own way of communicating its structure to employees. Some describe structure in their orientation or training programs, while others expect employees to learn from experience. Meetings, memos and procedure manuals often provide answers about formal structure. Two traditional means to communicate structure are organization charts and job descriptions.

Organization Charts

An organization chart diagrams the division of work responsibilities in a particular company. Organization charts show job functions by title and illustrate the direction of many communication channels by a graphic illustration of reporting relationships.

Figure 8.1 Organization Chart for Kiwaukee Savings and Loan Association

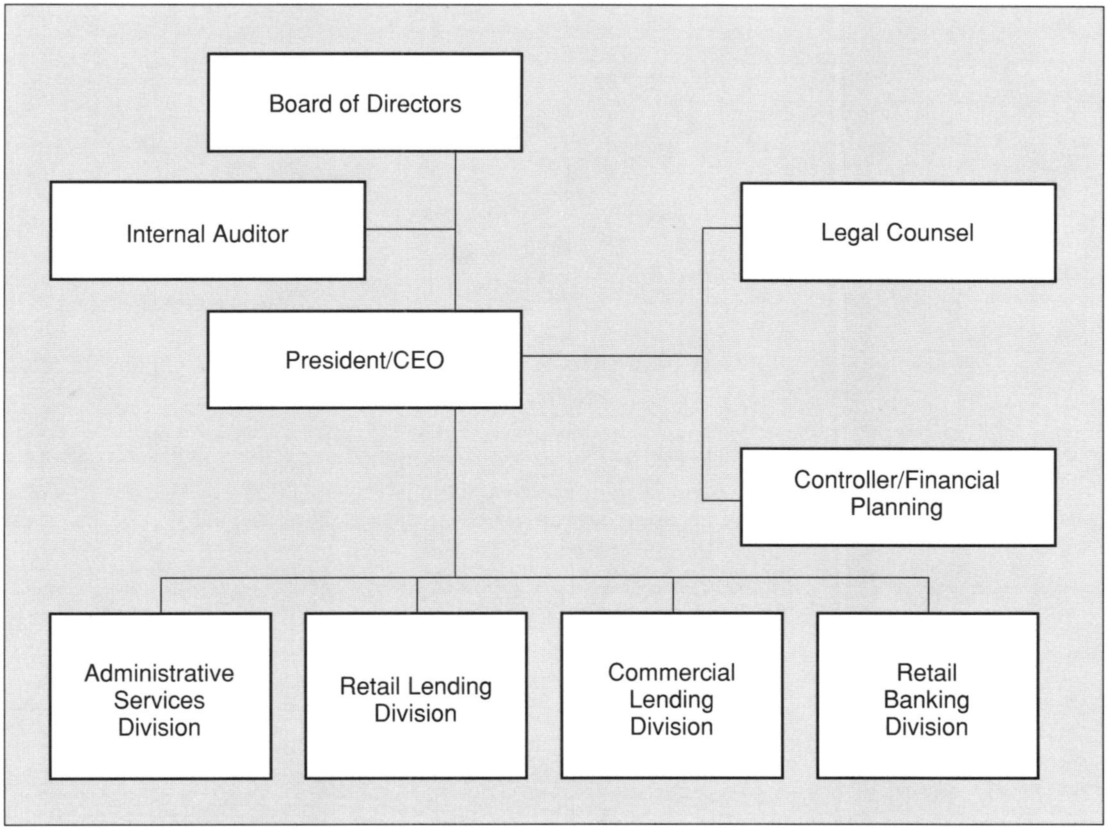

Figure 8.1 shows a portion of the organizational chart for Kiwaukee Savings and Loan Association. The solid vertical lines represent reporting relationships among entities. Notice, for instance, that the president and the internal auditor are the only two people who report directly to the board of directors. You can assume from this chart that only these two people communicate with board members regularly and extensively.

Four major work divisions at Kiwaukee shown in the figure are administrative services, retail lending, commercial lending and retail banking. The divisions' placement on the chart and the fact that all four titles are "division" show that they are of comparable importance to Kiwaukee's success as an organization. Each division, however, is assigned a specialized role in helping the organization meet its goals,

Figure 8.2 Retail Lending Division at Kiwaukee Savings and Loan Association

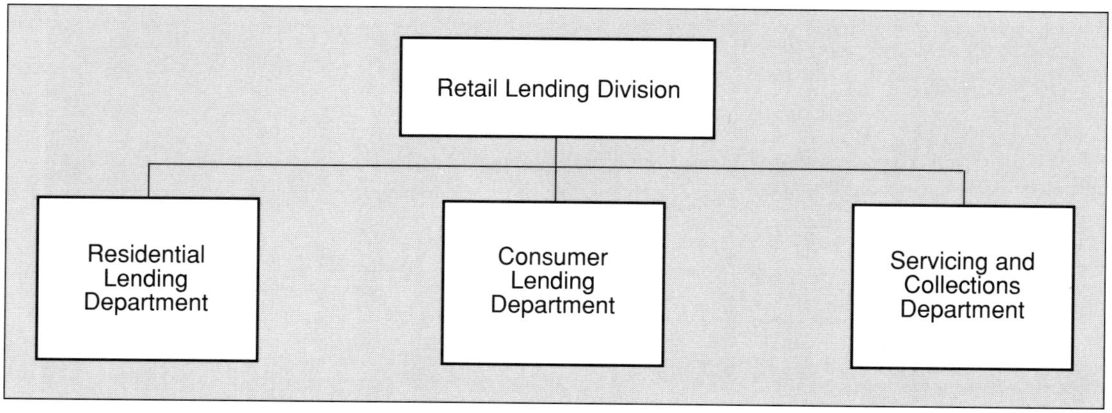

and the titles on the chart communicate these special roles. People within each division are apt to communicate most regularly with others in that group to coordinate efforts. To facilitate regular communication within the four work groups, Kiwaukee's offices are designed so that a division's work area is concentrated in one part of the building.

Figure 8.2 shows greater detail about one division, that of retail lending. Here the chart shows that the division's work is further divided into specialties: residential lending, consumer lending and loan servicing/collections, all called "departments." Within departments at this institution, communication is even more frequent. The people in the department all "talk the same language," so they can use acronyms or abbreviated messages that an outsider might not understand. Communication within these departments is also more casual and spontaneous, because the people know each other quite well and understand the demands of one another's jobs.

As you can see, the way Kiwaukee organizes its work strongly influences communication in the organization, and much of this can be learned from the organization chart. The chart also gives employees a sense of Kiwaukee's work division so that they know where to locate specialized information. The chart also demonstrates that, in order for Kiwaukee to operate, communication through formal channels must move up, down and horizontally.

Organization charts are only one tool for learning about communication in your organization. They convey the structure, but fail to show the communication due to friendships among staff members. They also do not reflect the regular communication that occurs between people whose work locations are close, even when work duties are not closely related.

Job Descriptions

Another way that organizational goals are communicated is through job descriptions. *Job descriptions*, as the name suggests, specify responsibilities of a particular position and name the reporting relationships of people who hold that job. With job descriptions the organization can explain work duties equitably because each description focuses on the job responsibilities rather than on any individual who holds the job. And, because they describe the full range of job duties, job descriptions clarify what is expected in an employee's performance. Figure 8.3 shows an example of a job description for a customer service representative position.

Job descriptions are a form of social communication. They can help new employees learn about the organization in a neutral and specific way. The boundaries they establish between a particular job and every other job also reduce uncertainty for all employees.

Like organization charts, job descriptions are a limited form of communication. Even the most complete description of your job would probably not include some of the events that make up your work day. Another limitation is that people may interpret the description about job requirements differently. Thus, job descriptions typically are only one way in which employees learn what they are expected to do.

Other Formal Methods

Businesses communicate structure through many other formal channels, especially when the information is likely to be useful for a long time or when it applies to a number of people. Structure can be communicated through written procedures manuals, annual reports and appraisal review procedures. Information in these communications will be used over a long period of time and will be relevant to many employees. Communication of this type tends to be precise and authoritative, so a written message or documentation is appropriate.

Other formal communication about structure occurs face-to-face. You learn about structure in meetings, from directions or explanations given by your supervisor, or through on-the-job training. Sometimes you learn about structure from questions you ask about a particular assignment. For example, you might learn that the accounting department needs you to supply information organized in a particular way because the data are forwarded to regulators. Sometimes an unwritten policy communicates structure, such as a policy that all inquiries about employment be referred to the human resources department.

You can learn still more about your institution's structure by nonverbal messages. Department members typically are placed close to-

Figure 8.3 Example of a Job Description

JOB DESCRIPTION	
JOB TITLE CUSTOMER SERVICE REPRESENTATIVE	**DATE** SEPTEMBER 1, 1989
DEPT/DIV RETAIL BANKING DIVISION	**GRADE** 10

GENERAL SUMMARY

The Customer Service Representative is responsible for performing the necessary customer service functions and operations included in the responsibilities named below and for active support of the institution's customer service policies. Performs under limited supervision and works as a team member to accomplish a common goal. Initiates action and demonstrates independent judgment.

PRINCIPAL DUTIES AND RESPONSIBILITIES

- Acknowledge customers in a friendly manner and be receptive to their needs. Promote to all customers the programs and services of the institution and endeavor to further the company's reputation for friendly, efficient and personal service.
- Demonstrate knowledge of the institution's current deposit and investment services. Listen actively and match customer's needs to appropriate services.
- Maintain daily balance of assigned cash drawer in accordance with cash control policies and procedures.
- Perform routine paying and receiving transaction services for customers.
- Maintain the confidentiality of all information related to customer accounts and affairs of the institution, and take actions needed to safeguard the assets of the institution and security of customer funds.
- Sell, redeem and maintain logs for money orders and traveler's checks.
- Provide personal service to customers by analyzing their needs and recommending the programs best suited to the customer's individual needs.
- Perform clerical support duties such as typing branch correspondence, filing and preparing reports as needed.
- Assist with other branch duties as assigned by supervisor or when necessary in order to complete day's work.

RELATIONSHIPS

Reports to assistant branch manager; may assist in training new CSRs.

gether to facilitate communication. Areas where the public has access, such as the teller and customer service areas, are neat and attractive to communicate a professional image. Status can also be deduced by work areas: a senior manager's office is usually more spacious than a junior manager's, for instance.

Structure sends organized, visible signals from a company to the people who work in it or use its services. From structure, you can understand much about the types of communication expected of you. A different set of messages about the organization is communicated through its culture.

Culture

Unlike structure, which can be identified clearly and objectively, culture is more intuitive than prescribed. It is seldom discussed or explained, and so is not highly visible. Yet a savings institution's culture profoundly affects the organization's success in reaching its goals.

Dictionaries define *culture* as a common pattern of human behavior within a group. The group tends to agree on basic values; therefore, group members share many beliefs and attitudes. These agreements result in unofficial rules regarding appropriate behavior for group members. In a business organization, culture can be summarized as "the way we do things around here."

Differences in Culture

Just as two organizations can operate with different structures, they can operate with different cultures as well. No single type of culture is inherently correct, but a company's culture should reflect and support the goals of the organization. If the culture is suited to meeting these goals, and if most employees appreciate and identify with the prevailing culture, the organization has a good chance of surviving and growing.

The following brief descriptions of First Savings and Second Savings illustrate different cultures. Observe that the differences between the basic beliefs communicated to employees affect their work procedures, rules and communication.

First Savings values tradition, cooperation and personalized customer service. Senior managers make most of the decisions and communicate them downward. First Savings is organized into a few broad work groups, with most people handling varied job duties. Staff members pitch in to help co-workers wherever needed. Helpfulness and teamwork are praised and rewarded. Because staff members work together frequently and need to know about a wide range of work topics, communication in First Savings is free-flowing and personal. Many procedural questions are answered informally.

In contrast, Second Savings takes pride in being up-to-the-minute, efficient and oriented to the "bottom line." While some decisions are handed down from the top, management at Second Savings frequently delegates decision-making authority and responsibility far down in the ranks. Second Savings is organized into departments with highly specialized assignments, and employees are expected to stay well informed in their specialties. Practical cost-trimming results are praised and rewarded. Because members of each specialized department have so much in common, communication is efficient; new techniques and procedures can be quickly determined and explained.

As these two examples show, the cultures are different but neither is "better" than the other. Neither pattern guarantees success of the business. Rather, the comparison illustrates different ways to operate a company in the business world based on different values, beliefs and attitudes. And, in each case, the institution's culture affects how people communicate.

Communicating Culture

Whatever beliefs they hold, business organizations benefit if their culture is strong and widely known. When this happens, most employees understand the company's goals and how their own roles help to achieve these goals without extensive formal communication and education from company management. Similar beliefs and attitudes lead to cooperative work systems and efficient communication.

In addition, a business with a strong culture tends to be stable. If everyone from the chairman of the board to the beginning teller sincerely believes in the same premise, such as that "the customer is always right" or "we're strong because we're lean and mean," rules and procedures don't need to be changed frequently. Across-the-board agreement reduces uncertainty, which in turn reduces the amount of communication needed to keep work moving as it should.

Finally, a strong culture clarifies expectations, both those of the organization toward its employees and of each employee toward management and co-workers. Suppose Highland Savings Bank's culture places a high value on innovation and setting trends. All employees who know this about the culture also know or quickly learn that this attitude requires them to be flexible, adaptive and willing to learn. Employees who know the culture *and* agree with it enjoy the excitement and challenge such a culture can bring. Their morale and loyalty are usually high because the company's values mirror their own.

The employees who do not understand Highland's cultural values or those who disapprove of them probably feel frustrated by the uncertainty and the temporary nature of their job assignments. It will be much harder for Highland to communicate with the second, resistant group because explanations and persuasion will need to be much more extensive. By contrast, communication among those who know and share the culture will be easier and more satisfying for both employees and management because everyone knows what to expect.

Summary

An organization is a group of people who join together to accomplish one or more tasks based on joint needs and expectations. Financial institutions are business organizations with the goal of providing financial services for a profit. As organizations, financial institutions agree on how tasks and responsibilities will be divided, establish goals and designate lines of authority. Overall, every member of a financial institution depends on everyone else to reach the agreed-on goals. Institutions need both good external and good internal communication to be sure everyone aims for the same goals.

Organizational communication is a coordinated and purposeful exchange of information and feelings among interdependent groups all directed toward the accomplishment of one or more major organizational goals. Communication permeates the business day and is a large factor in the success or failure of a business enterprise. Three important purposes of communication in a financial institution are to reach decisions, coordinate efforts and keep the organization functioning well.

The concept of communication flow explores how information moves from one part of the organization to another. One major method is through serial reproduction, when a message is transmitted from one person to another in a series of links. Serial reproduction poses problems to communicators, including leveling, sharpening and assimilating. A few ways to counteract these problems are limiting the number of links, sending a reasonable number of messages, limiting the amount of information in the message and reinforcing key points in the message.

Communication flows through financial institutions in formal, direct channels and informal channels. Formal channels are those planned for and supported by the institution. Informal channels include two general types: networks and the grapevine.

An organization communicates to employees and others visibly through its structure and in intangible ways through its culture. Samples of structural communication techniques are organization charts that describe the division and status of various jobs and job descriptions that provide guidelines on goals and responsibilities. Many other methods are common. Culture is a common pattern of behavior within a group based on common values and beliefs. In business, culture communicates messages on "how we do things around here." Business and employees benefit when their institution's culture is well defined, widely understood and broadly accepted.

Chapter Questions

1. Name the three purposes of organizational communication. How does each reflect the purposes of an organization?

2. What is serial reproduction? Name three risks involved with it.

3. Name four methods for overcoming the problems of serial reproduction.

4. Explain the major differences between formal and informal channels of communication.
5. How can informal communication through the grapevine be beneficial to an organization? How can it be detrimental?
6. Name four methods for overcoming the risks of informal communication.
7. Name three ways an organization conveys the idea of structure to its employees.
8. Why is communication enhanced when employees understand and adopt the culture of an organization?

FOOTNOTES

1. Stephen P. Robbins, *Management: Concepts and Problems* (Englewood Cliffs, N.J.: Prentice-Hall, 1984), p. 377.
2. "Labor Letter," *The Wall Street Journal*, February 16, 1988, p. 1.
3. Otis W. Baskin and Craig E. Aronoff, *Interpersonal Communications in Business* (Santa Monica, Calif.: Goodyear, 1980), p. 75.

Joe Munroe, Life Magazine © Time Inc.

"With three or more people, there is something bold in the air; direct things get said which frighten two people alone. . . . To be three is to be in public, you feel safe."

Elizabeth Bowden
The House in Paris *(1935)*

9 Small Group Communication

Objectives

After reading this chapter, you should be able to:

- Explain the differences between formal and informal groups, and give examples of each type as found in a typical savings institution;
- Define *task roles* and *maintenance roles*, and give four illustrations of each type;
- Give examples of individual and shared goals that are typical of groups in savings institutions;
- List three norms that can affect group communication in savings institutions;
- Define *cohesiveness* and explain how goals, norms and roles contribute to the cohesiveness of a group;
- Explain how an understanding of goals, norms and roles can help build better group communication;
- List three common barriers to group communication and suggest several strategies to overcome each.

A MAJOR PART OF BUSINESS COMMUNICATION takes place in groups. Consider some typical groups that claim your membership as a financial institution employee: the financial institution itself, the particular branch where you work, your department in the institution (loan servicing, customer service, data processing, etc.), your lunch and coffee-break companions, a Christmas party planning committee, a softball or bowling team. Any organization can be viewed as groups of individuals who are seeking to satisfy individual and collective goals.

Regardless of the reasons for their existence, at least one common thread runs through all groups. When a collection of people is assembled, inevitably those people will collect, process and produce information. Groups play a pivotal role in the communication process within an organization. And in situations where decision making or information gathering can be enhanced by input from a variety of sources, effective group communication is essential to an organization.

Group communication uses all the elements of communication that you have studied so far, but it employs those elements in a unique and slightly more complex way. When you belong to a group, you continue to communicate intrapersonally and interpersonally—as does each of the other group members. But something else happens as well. You begin to communicate with more than one person at the same time. The people in the group around you become an audience. Perceptions, word meanings and nonverbal symbols become much more varied. The number of messages sent and received increases. Listening skills must become more intensely focused. In short, the group setting adds more complexity to the already complicated process of communication.

This chapter explores groups in a financial institution setting—their composition, their dynamics and their role in communication. It also describes barriers that can block communication and suggests ways that you can overcome those barriers and communicate more effectively in small groups within your institution.

Types of Groups in an Organization

A group consists of three or more—but generally less than 15—people who share a common purpose or goal. This definition can incorporate both a highly structured group, such as the six members of a loan servicing department, and a more informal collection of individuals, such as four employees who regularly meet for coffee and lunch. Each is a collection of three or more people. In each, the individual members share a common purpose or goal: the loan servicing department, to foster the aims and objectives of their department; the lunch group, to socialize. In general, there are two major types of groups: formal and informal.

Formal Groups

Formal groups consist of individuals who are brought together by the organization to accomplish specific tasks within departments or divisions of the institution. People are frequently assigned to a formal group because of their position in the organization, or because they possess a specific skill or knowledge the group needs. For example, members of a loan servicing department are part of this formal group because of their positions with the institution. An institution's Christmas party committee, on the other hand, may consist of individuals from various departments or levels who were assigned because previous experience has given them expertise in organizing or planning.

Formal groups meet during work hours to accomplish organizational or departmental objectives. Formal groups also typically adhere to carefully structured plans and procedures for accomplishing a designated task.

A wide variety of formal groups exists within financial institutions. A number of these groups, such as the auditing staff, the consumer lending department, the loan servicing department, or the savings department, are actually built into the structure of the institution. Members of these groups share departmental goals that contribute to the overall aims and goals of the institution.

Other formal groups within a financial institution may be less permanent and may be organized by management as the need arises. For example, decision-making teams, problem-solving groups or quality circles convene to tackle specific issues and then disband after they have accomplished their tasks. Even though the purposes or goals of such ad hoc committees may differ, these groups all share similar patterns of communication: members gather and share information, pool ideas, evaluate those ideas and make decisions.

Decision-making teams might consist of department members or representatives from various departments who collect information, evaluate that information and make a recommendation that affects the procedures or operations of the organization. Similarly, problem-solving groups study an identified problem related to operations, suggest possible solutions for the problem, evaluate those solutions and recommend action. Quality circles typically involve members from a variety of departments and levels within an organization. These groups evaluate organizational operations or products, brainstorm possible alternatives or revisions, and suggest ways to improve the quality of services or products.

Informal Groups

Informal groups are created by individuals who come together because of common needs, interests or concerns. Unlike formal groups, they are not officially established by the organization, and their leaders have no official authority as group representative. An informal group typically does not rely on established or structured plans and procedures to accomplish its tasks. Additionally, the tasks often have personal as well as professional objectives. Examples of informal groups in a financial institution include tellers who regularly take coffee breaks together, employees from different departments who commute together each morning, or employees who regularly go out for dinner or play softball after work.

A primary function of informal groups in an organization is the formation of friendships. Through activities such as lunches, regular card games, bowling or softball games, individual group members satisfy their social needs as they get to know one another.

In addition, informal groups can contribute to the effective operation of an institution. For example, a group of employees from different departments who socialize regularly during lunch periods may devise and suggest new ways to facilitate the flow of transactions from department to department. Or members of one department who regularly carpool to and from work may share information on new policies and procedures, or offer suggestions on ways to improve job performance within the department.

Informal groups can also serve as important pressure groups or political alliances within a department and within the institution. A group of tellers may decide during their after-work gatherings that an employee needs extra help fitting into the department. Over dinner and bowling, the tellers can devise plans for taking the new person in hand and "teaching her the ropes." Or the same tellers may use the informal group to develop plans for pressuring other department members into revising lunch hour or break schedules.

No matter what position you hold in a financial institution, much of your work day involves interaction with groups of one kind or another. Because these groups provide the setting for so much on-the-job communication, you can improve your ability as a communicator by understanding the composition and characteristics of groups. Four characteristics common to all groups are cohesiveness, goals, norms and roles.

COHESIVENESS

For any group to function effectively, its members need to feel a sense of interdependence; they need to think of themselves as a group rather than as separate individuals. In other words, a group must be cohesive in order to be effective. *Cohesiveness* can be defined as the sense of loyalty toward other members of the group or toward the group itself.

Members of a cohesive group reflect the Three Musketeers' motto, "All for one and one for all." This spirit of cohesiveness can be illustrated by tellers who help one another balance at the end of the day so that the job gets done and no one has to stay late.

Cohesiveness in any group results directly from common goals, shared norms and clearly defined roles. In other words, groups become cohesive when their members share and work toward the same goals, operate by the same norms or standards, and understand and feel comfortable about their roles in the group. An organization's Christmas party committee becomes cohesive when its members agree on what they want to accomplish in their planning, when they share the same values and beliefs about the best style of operation, and when members are clear about and comfortable with their tasks in the meetings and in the preparations.

Conversely, cohesiveness is destroyed or weakened when individuals do not subscribe to the goals of the group, when members do not understand or operate within the group norms, or when important roles go unfilled or become blurred. In the Christmas party committee example, group cohesiveness would be damaged if half the group felt the party should provide an informal opportunity for employees to mix and converse, while the other half wanted entertainment in which employees were merely an audience. Likewise, the cohesiveness of the committee would be weakened if members disagreed over how their planning meetings should be run, if key individuals were unwilling or unable to provide information or ideas in the meetings, or if members were unhappy with their tasks in preparing for the party.

Cohesiveness is also a key factor in fostering effective group communication. When individuals feel a sense of group loyalty and interdependence, they generally communicate effectively with one another. Since cohesiveness results from shared goals and norms and from clearly defined and accepted roles, we will use these elements to explore strategies that foster group cohesiveness.

Goals

A characteristic basic to all groups—the element that draws individuals into a group—is goals or objectives. People form groups to accomplish something. These goals are of two types: shared goals and individual goals.

Shared Goals

Shared goals are the aims or objectives of the entire group. For most informal groups, shared goals are implicit, but are not usually written down. Employees who regularly eat lunch or bowl together, for example, will not have written statements of objectives for their groups. However, if such groups were questioned about their goals, members

would probably agree on such objectives as to socialize, to get to know one another or to have fun.

In formal groups, such as a department within a financial institution, shared goals are often spelled out in procedures manuals for new employees or conveyed verbally by supervisors in department meetings. Such statements of objectives are often referred to as the group's *charge*. The charge usually includes the organization's expectations of the group, the duties of group members, criteria for membership, the group's relationship with other groups in the institution and reporting procedures for group members.

Formal groups can increase their cohesiveness by making certain that such group goals are clearly defined and understood by all members. Research indicates that there is a direct relationship between clearly defined goals and cohesiveness among group members.[1] To increase understanding of shared goals, a supervisor can use a department meeting to expand on reasons for the goals, explain how those goals complement the overall goals of the institution, describe each employee's role in helping to achieve the goals, and invite questions and comments from individuals within the department. Such give-and-take among department members not only clarifies goals, but also allows each individual to develop a personal stake in and commitment to the goals.

In addition, supervisors can regularly review and assess progress toward goals in a group setting. When a group realizes its progress toward achieving its goals, its members' cohesiveness grows stronger; when progress is stalled, cohesiveness decreases. Periodic progress checks give the group a chance to review and, if necessary, to adjust the goals, to break them into smaller, more attainable segments, or to develop a more effective strategy for reaching them. Such interaction also increases group commitment to the goals and fosters healthy group communication.

Individual Goals

Within any group, there may be as many individual goals as there are group members. *Individual goals* are the aims and objectives of individual members. Each person brings to a group his or her unique objectives and expectations. For example, one person may decide to work at a savings institution to get a background in finance, while another person may choose the job simply because it offers a regular paycheck. One person may choose to be a teller to gain a broad understanding of the institution's operations, while someone else sees the job as a chance to interact with customers.

Individual goals for group membership are generally either task-related objectives (How can this group help me improve my skills? Foster my chances for promotion? Improve my quality of life?) or social goals (How can the group improve my sense of belonging? Satisfy my need for controlling others? Supply feelings of care and affection?). Most people join groups to fulfill both task-related objectives and social goals. A person might volunteer to serve on a financial institution's newsletter staff, for example, to learn about the business of finance, to achieve recognition and to develop new friendships.

Sometimes an individual's goals correlate closely to the goals of the group. A teller's individual goal of learning the business or helping customers, for instance, supports her department's goals of increasing deposits or gaining new accounts. In groups where individual and shared goals are similar or compatible, communication between members is enhanced. People who share similar goals are more likely to share information, ideas and suggestions that facilitate those goals. However, in groups where individuals' goals are incompatible with or markedly different from the group's goals, communication between members may become strained.

Norms

Norms are shared values and beliefs about how people in a group should behave toward one another. Group values and beliefs develop over time as the result of repetition and tradition. These unwritten rules provide standards for communication among group members, between members and group leaders or superiors, and with individuals who are outside the group. For example, consider some of the following norms that may affect communication in your department or financial institution:

- In department meetings, the supervisor will speak first and then allow questions.

- Open expressions of hostility or disagreement are not permitted in the presence of customers.
- In work settings where several employees are bilingual, English is the preferred spoken language.
- Topics such as job dissatisfaction or strained relations between co-workers are not discussed when the supervisor is present.
- During lunch breaks, it is generally not acceptable to invite "outsiders" to join in the group conversation.

Some differences in attitudes and behavior among group members are acceptable and even beneficial to a group, but if the members' understanding of acceptable values and beliefs varies widely, the group's cohesiveness and communication will suffer. If enough members hold divergent views about acceptable group behavior, the group will cease to function effectively. If group norms are particularly strong, it is usually because individuals agree completely with the group's goals and value system or because they do not want to be ostracized from the group.

For example, consider the potential problems of the following situation in which a group norm is transgressed. The customer contact staff at United Federal follow an unwritten rule that employees do not express annoyances or problems with customers in the presence of management. A recently hired employee is unaware of this norm. During several lunch hours this past week, Sheila, a new accounts counselor, complained and joked about obnoxious customers while Brad Sawyer, the department supervisor, was in the cafeteria. The other employees at Sheila's table grew quiet and nervously toyed with their food, refusing to respond to Sheila's remarks. Shortly after Brad left the cafeteria, these employees excused themselves and left Sheila to finish her lunch alone.

In this situation, the other group members have the responsibility of communicating expectations to persons who do not conform to norms. The employees at United Federal used nonverbal communication—their silence and withdrawal—to express disapproval to Sheila. Such nonverbal cues are one way of bringing individuals into conformity with norms and, thereby, indirectly communicating group norms. However, for the communication to be effective, the nonconformists must be alert and receptive to the nonverbal cues.

Another subtle but more direct method of communicating norms is the use of humor to apply pressure to nonconforming individuals. For example, one of Sheila's companions might joke with Sheila later in the restroom: "Hey, you may have spoiled Mr. Sawyer's lunch today. Supervisors get upset stomachs when they hear bad things about customers."

Reprinted by permission of UFS, Inc.

All forms of humor can serve as a corrective mechanism. Humor creates and releases tension at the same time. By using humor, you can tell deviating members that the group disapproves of their behavior in a such a way as to elicit a laugh, which releases the tension.

If strategies such as nonverbal cues and humor fail to work, group members may need to resort to more direct efforts. By the use of persuasive or even coercive confrontations, group representatives can alert the nonconformist to the group's concern about his or her behavior. However, it is important to remember that such confrontations are most effective when they are handled in a way that respects the individual's dignity and demonstrates genuine empathy. If Sheila fails to recognize her co-workers' nonverbal cues and the messages cloaked in humor, her co-workers might choose a discreet time and place to use a more direct approach: "Sheila, we can see how you would be irritated with some customers. We all have to deal with difficult people at times, and we've all griped to each other. But around here, we just don't complain about customers in front of management."

Roles

Within any group, each member has a specific role to play. Just as norms define acceptable group standards and values, *roles* refer to the patterns of behavior expected of the individual members.[2] Group roles are determined by the expectations of other group members, nongroup members and each individual.

Some roles, especially in formal groups, carry labels or titles such as "supervisor," "chairperson," "manager," "employee" or "student".

Other roles are untitled and unassigned, but just as real. For example, some members of groups are clearly followers and others are leaders, even though these roles are rarely discussed or acknowledged. Such untitled roles define the function and identity of individuals within the group and have an effect on group communication. An understanding of these untitled functional roles can help to explain why any group does or does not communicate successfully, and enables group members to reduce role problems and strengthen cohesiveness. Functional roles fall into two categories: task roles and maintenance roles.

Task Roles

As discussed earlier, every group has objectives or goals to accomplish. In order to accomplish these goals, group members must participate and communicate in ways that focus on getting the group's task done. *Task roles* describe the functions and behavior of group members that contribute to accomplishing the group's task. For example, if a group's task is to assess the effectiveness of a new account entry system, one member will need to organize and head the group, while other members will need to gather data, summarize and evaluate the information, and suggest ideas.

Task roles are not mutually exclusive; a given individual may play several roles at any one time, and one role may be played by various group members. Some of the most important task roles in any group include initiator, contributor, coordinator, evaluator, summarizer and energizer.

Initiator. The initiator triggers group interaction by setting agendas, defining problems and suggesting new ideas for group consideration. In a savings institution, an initiator may be the teller supervisor who calls a department meeting to announce a new computerized system for deposit accounts. Another example is the data processor who suggests to the members of his or her lunch group that they begin meeting after work for a weekly softball game.

Contributor. Every group needs individuals who contribute ideas, information and opinions related to the group's task. In a department meeting, contributors may provide results from a recent audit, or they may suggest ways to streamline deposit procedures or record keeping. In a Christmas party committee meeting, a contributor may report on staff reactions to the previous year's decorations or provide ideas for new music and refreshments for this year's party.

Coordinator. Coordinators help to clarify various positions that other group members have expressed on issues or tasks. They may also clarify relationships among information, ideas, and opinions, or suggest ways to integrate divergent positions. For example, a group member acts as coordinator when, during a weekly meeting with other tellers, he says, "Liza, you say the new deposit slips create more problems than the old ones. Jim thinks they're great. Why don't you tell us about some of the problems, and let's see how Jim would handle them?"

Evaluator. The evaluator, or critic, helps the group stay inside the boundaries of its standards or norms. An evaluator may also raise important questions about the logic, practicality or morality of the group's actions or plans. If a financial institution's public relations department decided to hold a public raffle or bingo game to publicize the opening of a new building addition, an evaluator might question whether such events are consistent with the institution's role of encouraging money management.

Summarizer. A group needs members who can summarize what occurred—either in its meetings or in its efforts to reach goals—and point out how successful the group has been or how far from the goal the group has strayed. At the end of a department meeting, for example, a summarizer would reiterate the points that were covered, highlighting any major decisions or suggestions.

Energizer. Finally, individuals who prod the group to action fulfill the role of energizer. This role is especially useful at times when the group gets off the track, strays from its objectives or begins to lose interest. Energizers may encourage group action with words such as, "Let's make a decision or move on; we've been on this point long enough," or "Hey, if the loan servicing department can do it, so can we!"

Maintenance Roles

To function effectively, any group needs an environment in which members communicate well by sharing ideas, accepting diverse opinions and managing conflict. In order to foster and maintain such a productive group environment, individual members assume *maintenance roles.* These roles keep relationships among members running smoothly and protect the cohesiveness of the group. Among the maintenance roles played by group members are supporter/encourager, harmonizer, tension reliever, compromiser, gatekeeper and follower.

Supporter/Encourager Group members play the role of supporter/encourager by praising and openly agreeing with others' contributions ("That's a great suggestion, Juanita!") and by recognizing and encouraging fellow members' ideas and suggestions ("I think Carl's idea about changing the computer program would really help. Why don't we let him elaborate on it?").

Harmonizer. The harmonizer reconciles disagreements and disputes among other group members. Often, such an individual tries to help the differing parties explain their position to each other: "I think your ideas aren't really all that different. You both seem to want a better method of scheduling lunch hours. Jodie, are you saying . . .? And, Lynne, do you mean . . .?"

Tension Reliever. Persons who assume the role of tension reliever are assets to any group. These members use wit and humor to defuse tense situations and relax the group. For example, if a department meeting has begun to degenerate into a heated conflict of opinions, a tension reliever might interject: "Hey, we'd better move away from the sprinkler system. At the rate we're heating up, that thing is going to go off in a minute."

Compromiser. Compromisers admit the possibility of error or give in on issues when they are involved in conflict with other group members. For example, when a conflict arises over plans for locating new computer equipment in the loan servicing department, a compromiser might suggest, "Well, I didn't really want to have the printer that close to my desk, but maybe it wouldn't be too bad if we move a partition to muffle some of the noise."

Gatekeeper. The gatekeeper facilitates interaction among group members. Gatekeepers keep communication channels open and encourage contributions from members who are usually silent: "Valencia, you look like you've been thinking a lot about this. What is your opinion of Tom's suggestion?"

Follower. Followers go along with the general attitude of the group, are open to and accepting of others' ideas and suggestions, and are willing to assume tasks the group assigns them. Followers rarely desire to play the role of "leader" and often serve as an audience to group interaction.

Groups function best and communicate most effectively when these important group roles are filled and when all members know and feel comfortable with their roles. When important roles remain unfilled, when members are uncertain about the boundaries of their roles, or when there is unhealthy competition for roles, the cohesiveness of the group will suffer.

Assignment of Roles

Most group members are unaware of the existence of functional roles. Individuals in groups generally will not say, "You provide support and encouragement, I'll offer information, and he can be the energizer." Over time, however, certain members begin to assume specific roles, for two reasons. First, persons often assume roles that are compatible with their individual personalities, skills and interests. For example, some individuals are more skilled in organizing or understanding the overall picture. These people may quite naturally take the role of evaluators or summarizers. Group members who are sensitive to the emotions and reactions of co-workers, or who are skilled at settling disputes and differences, may take the roles of supporter or harmonizer.

In addition to the personalities and skills of group members, the needs of the group may determine the roles that individuals play. If an important role, such as initiator, contributor, or supporter, goes unfilled, the group may have difficulty working cohesively toward its goal. In the case of such *role vacuums*, group members may take on roles they would not ordinarily assume, simply because of the group's need. For example, persons who are not generally critical may become evaluators in a group where no one else is performing this important task. If a group's discussion has stalled because no one is contributing ideas or supplying necessary information, a normally withdrawn member may suddenly take on the role of contributor. Or someone who is usually critical or argumentative may find it necessary to act as harmonizer when disputes between members with opposing viewpoints prevent progress.

When role vacuums occur, group members must be alert and perceptive enough to recognize the problem and then act to fill the vacuums. In many cases, the group leader can easily initiate such action by delegating specific roles to individual members: "Jeff, you've done quite a lot of work with opening accounts; could you describe some of the problems you've had with our new account forms?" Or: "Lavonne, you're usually pretty good at seeing both sides of an issue. Can you suggest a way that we might be able to use both Kim's and Victor's suggestions?"

Coordinating Roles

Group members need to feel secure and clear about the roles they play within a group. Competition for the same role can threaten members' feelings of group status, lead to jealousy and insecurity, and hinder the group's progress in its tasks. For example, imagine a group in which members are vying for the role of tension reliever. Such competition may result in clowns who are trying to top each other in getting laughs while, at the same time, distracting the group from accomplishing its goal.

Role competition often exists in groups, but in some cases it may be imagined by insecure members who are uncertain about the extent or boundaries of their roles. In either case, the group must manage the problem to restore cohesiveness. Group leaders are probably in the best position to define and coordinate roles. Often, the leader can squelch role competition simply by targeting a role to one individual: "Juan, you're good at summarizing. How about giving us a recap of what we've just covered?" However, at times the leader may need to direct an individual into a different or more constructive role: "Laura, the way you're joking about this suggestion seems to indicate that you don't feel it's going to work. How would you suggest we approach the problem?"

Group roles may change or shift as situations and individuals change. However, to protect cohesiveness, all group members must become sensitive to the roles that exist in their group and alert themselves to indications that they may have overstepped their role or that they are trespassing on another's territory.

Group Communication Barriers and Strategies

Even when much attention is given to building group cohesiveness by spelling out objectives, clarifying norms and solidifying roles, communication problems will invariably arise within any group. Three barriers typically threaten group communication: conflict, agendas and "groupthink". While these barriers may arise at any time, the unique structure and components of a group can be used to overcome each of them.

Conflict

Because a group consists of individuals with different values, experiences, perceptions and listening skills, it is quite natural that conflicts will arise within the group. Four types of conflict are typical in group interaction: affective conflict, procedural conflict, substantive conflict and inequity conflict.

Affective conflict results from personality clashes between individuals. For example, if you are in a group with someone you don't like, you may experience conflicts that have nothing to do with the group's goals or procedures. Such interpersonal conflicts are not caused by the group structure, but because they occur within and affect the group, they must be considered group conflicts.

Procedural conflict is, as its name indicates, disagreement over group procedures or methods. As an illustration, consider the Christmas party planning committee whose goal is to provide party entertainment that all the employees will enjoy. Several members of the group want to create a questionnaire and poll employees about their choice of entertainment. Several other members feel that a poll would take too long;

they want to make the decision themselves as representatives of the employees.

Substantive conflict involves disagreement over ideas, information, reasoning or evidence that is shared within the group. Members of a loan committee, for example, may disagree in their evaluations of the data on a mortgage loan application. Several members may feel the data indicates that the applicant is a safe investment, while others believe that he or she is too much of a risk.

Finally, *inequity conflict* is disagreement over perceived unequal workloads or contributions of individuals in the group. Inequity conflicts are fairly common among work groups or departments in which some employees feel that they have been assigned "the worst hours" or "the hardest jobs," or that some employees in the department "just aren't pulling their weight."

Conflict as a Positive Factor

Some people mistakenly think that conflict is always bad and should be avoided at any cost. As Chapter 7 explained, conflict can provide an opportunity to identify, clarify and solve problems or resolve differences. In group situations, conflict can also encourage and bolster the involvement of group members. For example, when several individuals in a group express opposing viewpoints over procedures, information, workloads, or even group goals, other group members are forced to recognize the issues, to assess the opposing viewpoints and to clarify their own feelings on the issues. Conflict can also produce better group decisions when it spurs members to scrutinize and question the issues under consideration. When conflict can engender this kind of involvement, it becomes a real asset to group communication.

Conflict as a Barrier

As long as group disagreements center in procedures, ideas, information and workloads, conflict can be a healthy force in group interaction. However, when disagreements stem from the personal differences of individuals within the group, conflict can destroy relationships and interaction. When group members disagree with one another simply because they hold different values or perceptions, they can become involved in conflicts that detract from the group goals and objectives. Personality conflicts are especially dangerous because they often spill over into issues that affect the entire group.

For instance, Mark may have a personality conflict with Jan because Jan has unwittingly made flippant remarks about Mark's involvement in church groups. During department meetings to discuss methods to implement a new training program, Mark may carry over his dislike for Jan and, consequently, ridicule or object to her suggestions for training without really considering their worth.

Because they divert the group from issues that relate to its goals, personality conflicts can destroy the cohesiveness and effectiveness of the group. However, by observing several helpful communication guidelines, you can minimize the dangers of such negative conflict.

Be Aware of Differences. Although it sounds obvious, one of the keys to minimizing destructive conflict is simply to acknowledge the differences that exist within the group. Groups are collections of individuals, and each individual is unique. The people who make up a group come from different backgrounds. These differences will be exhibited in countless ways. A joke that is humorous to one member may be offensive to another. A department directive that seems concise and "no-nonsense" to one individual may seem dictatorial and unfeeling to another. To be an effective communicator in groups, you must not only acknowledge that such differences are natural, but that they can add a beneficial variety of perspectives to the group.

Stay Open-Minded. Because different personalities, values and priorities exist in any group, it helps to remain objective when you approach group interaction. As much as possible, put aside your prejudices or personal disagreements and try to focus on the goals and objectives of the group: "Will this suggestion or plan help us to meet our goal?" If it is not possible to put aside your personal prejudices, at least be aware of their influence on your judgment as you consider suggestions or contributions of other group members.

Listen Carefully. In any group setting, participants need to give careful attention to the contributions of *all* members. This means that you must listen as carefully to those individuals whom you dislike as to those whom you like. Focus on the ideas and information, not just the speaker. Ask questions about language that may be unclear or confusing. Observe nonverbal cues and reactions of other listeners to see how the speaker's contribution affects the entire group. Provide feedback by paraphrasing information in clear and objective terms. Such objective feedback may be especially helpful if you sense that the speaker has irritated other group members through the use of biased or "loaded" language. For instance, you may sense tension in a Christmas party planning meeting after a member has suggested that you play "fun music and not just that religious stuff." You may be able to soothe any irritation created by such loaded language simply by paraphrasing the suggestion in a more objective manner: "You're saying that it would be good to have both secular and religious Christmas music?"

Use Empathy. Conflict can also be soothed when you try to understand the thoughts and feelings of all the group members. If you are aware of the values that motivate other individuals in the group, you will be better equipped to understand their contributions and more effective at expressing your ideas to them. For example, consider a deposit accounts department in which an older employee is especially sensitive about his age and another employee is devoted to her elderly, retired father. An awareness of these individuals' feelings can help you curb expressions of impatience or annoyance when discussing problems caused by retired customers who forget to sign Social Security checks or who fill out deposit slips incorrectly. For example, you would avoid using expressions such as "forgetful old people," which might upset these employees and lead to conflicts.

Draw on the Structure of the Group. When you sense that personality conflicts are interfering with group interaction and effective functioning, you can use the goals, norms and roles of the group to curtail the conflicts. For instance, conflict can be avoided by tactfully interrupting an interpersonal conflict between two individuals and recalling the group's objective: "I wonder if this disagreement is really going to help us plan a way to reach our sales quota this month." You might also apply group pressure by collectively ignoring the conflicting parties, or gently apply humor to the situation to remind conflicting members of communication norms that do not allow for lengthy personal disputes.

Finally, you might need to assume the role of harmonizer to resolve the dispute and get on with the business of the group: "I'm sure you both want to come up with a good plan for the group, but you seem to be stuck on the wording of this suggestion. I wonder if we couldn't incorporate both of your ideas by . . ."

Agendas

In addition to conflict, agendas can also be a potential barrier to effective group communication. An *agenda* is an established, orderly procedure that outlines processes to follow to reach objectives or goals. An agenda is usually formulated by the group leader, who presents it to the group orally or in written form. Agendas can vary depending on the group, the purpose of the meeting or project, and the preferences of the group leader. They can be simply structured, listing a few goals to be reached within an established time frame, or they can be more complex. Figure 9.1 illustrates the basic pattern followed in a problem-solving agenda. This agenda provides an outline of the tasks that need to be accomplished to solve a problem. Just as conflict can both enhance and hinder interaction in a group, an agenda can be both a benefit and a barrier to group communication.

Benefits of Agendas

As Figure 9.1 illustrates, agendas can provide an orderly framework to facilitate group efforts. When they are carefully and thoughtfully con-

Figure 9.1 Problem Solving Agenda

AGENDA

1. Present the group goal in a way that is clear to all group members.
2. State the problem or issue that must be dealt with in order to reach the goal.
3. Assemble facts and information needed.
4. Establish criteria by which to evaluate the assembled information.
5. Generate a list of suggested solutions or strategies.
6. Evaluate the solutions on the basis of established criteria.
7. Choose the solution that will best achieve the objective.

structed, agendas are invaluable tools for effective group interaction. They give groups a clear sense of direction, and they enable members to prepare for and participate in orderly steps toward reaching the group's goals. Agendas can provide structure to a single meeting or to longer-term projects—such as departmental programs to increase deposit accounts or to sell new types of CDs—that involve various forms of group interaction.

Agendas as Barriers

Although agendas aid the effective functioning of most groups, agendas can also create communication problems when they become too rigid or when they are followed slavishly. If patterns of communication become too rigid and controlled, creative ideas and impromptu suggestions may be ignored or lost simply because they "should have been mentioned last week" or "we're not at that point on the agenda yet."

In addition, agendas that are established without any input from the group members have the disadvantage of seeming to be "handed down from above." Group members may resent being left out of the initial stages of setting group goals and procedures. Because they do not feel a sense of ownership in the agenda, members may be less enthused about following it or contributing to the procedures it outlines.

Finally, agendas can create communication barriers if group members always feel constrained to confine their remarks and contributions to the "business at hand." You have probably experienced meetings or working conditions in which casual conversations or spontaneous interactions with co-workers were frowned on. Such constraints can thwart interpersonal relations among individuals and build tension and resentment in the group.

Barriers such as these can be avoided if agendas are handled with flexibility and a sensitivity to group feelings and moods. If it is possible and appropriate, group members might help formulate goals—or at least address questions and concerns about the goals. Group leaders and members should feel free to interrupt the agenda with important questions or suggestions at any point in the procedure. Agendas should also be flexible enough to allow occasional spontaneous exchanges or "off-the-subject" contributions from members. Such diversions can actually contribute to the group's progress by building cohesiveness between members, relieving tension and, at times, giving the group a fresh perspective on its task.

Hidden Agendas

Hidden agendas are not agendas in the sense that we have been using the term, that is, they are not procedures for accomplishing group objectives. In small group communication, a *hidden agenda* is a group member's personal tasks that may conflict with the group task. They are agendas because they usually involve procedures for achieving individual goals, and they are "hidden" because they are often not known to other group members.

Hidden agendas can create serious problems for effective group functioning. As mentioned earlier in this chapter, group cohesion and communication can suffer when an individual's goals differ from the goals of the group. For example, a data processor whose chief goal is to learn the capacity of various pieces of equipment and then move on to "bigger and better positions" may fail to do his part in completing the department's monthly account entries because he is "getting to know the machines." In such a situation, the employee's hidden agenda may create tension and resentment among other department members.

The most effective way to deal with hidden agendas is to uncover or identify them. When other group members observe signs of a hidden agenda in a co-worker's activities or contributions, they need to point out their discoveries and limit the influence of the hidden agenda on the group's activities. By making individuals aware that you have discovered their hidden agendas, you can often effectively curtail their strategies and minimize the negative effects of hidden agendas on the group.

For example, consider the case of the data processor who is more concerned about learning the capacity of the equipment than completing his share of department duties. Several co-workers who have recognized his hidden agenda might approach him tactfully about their discovery ("Mitch, we know you like to experiment with the equipment, and it looks like you're really getting good at it . . .") and then minimize the effects of the hidden agenda by focusing on group objectives (". . . but we do have department deadlines, you know, and when you don't get your work done, the rest of us have to pick up the slack.").

When dealing with hidden agendas, it is important to be realistic and reasonable. You cannot expect a person to reject all of his or her personal goals for the good of the group. It is often helpful to acknowledge the value of an individual's agenda and, if possible, suggest a compromise that will not require the person to relinquish personal goals completely. In the illustration of the data processor, for example, the other group members acknowledged the value of his agenda ("it looks like you're really getting good at it"). They might also want to suggest a strategy that will allow him to pursue his goal in a way that will not damage the group: "Why don't you find out if you can come in early or stay after work some nights to play around with the equipment?"

Groupthink

Up to this point, cohesiveness has been expressed as an important factor in effective group interaction and communication. However, as with conflict and agendas, there is a negative side to group cohesiveness. When cohesiveness stifles thinking or encourages mindless assent to "whatever the group wants to do," it can damage communication and threaten effective group functioning. This negative side to cohesiveness is called groupthink. *Groupthink* is the tendency of highly cohesive groups to conform to ideas or approaches simply because the members sense that "this is what the group wants." Groupthink occurs when a group has met together for a while and its members have developed a way of thinking within the group that decreases their objectivity and openness to new and divergent viewpoints.

A classic illustration of this phenomenon is a study in which college students were shown three lines of different lengths and asked to identify which of them matched a fourth line. The correct answer was obvious. However, all but one person in each experimental group had been instructed to vote for the wrong line. As a result, a third of the uninformed subjects voted with the majority, ignoring their own judgment.[3] This tendency to "go with the group" at the expense of individuality or personal judgment is the hallmark of groupthink, and it can result in serious communication problems within groups.

Effects on Communication

Groupthink can result in two serious communication problems. First, individuals in the group become reluctant to express objections to any ideas or suggestions of others. To express such dissenting views once groupthink has taken hold might be viewed as disloyalty to the group or to the members whose ideas are criticized: "I don't want to make her think I'm a troublemaker; and besides, I'm probably the only one who has problems with the plan." This self-censorship discourages independent, objective thinking and healthy conflict.

The second communication problem created by groupthink is that individuals within the group often blindly accept any group proposals as good or beneficial without attempting to examine them carefully. They ignore the advantages—and even the disadvantages—of any alternatives. When taken to its extreme, groupthink can cause group members to feel invulnerable and infallible. This tunnel vision can be illustrated by a financial institution that chooses to do things "the way we always have," despite customer suggestions and complaints and in disregard of threats from competing institutions.

Minimizing the Effects of Groupthink

How can groupthink be avoided without damaging healthy group cohesiveness? The following suggestions can encourage group interaction and, at the same time, minimize the effects of groupthink.

Be Open to Disagreement. The group leader or an appropriate group member can promote an atmosphere in which everyone feels free to disagree. Leaders can set a tone that encourages openness and dissension, or they can call on the "evaluators" in the group to play devil's advocate on important or controversial issues. The tension-reliever or group comedian may encourage healthy dissension with a pointed but good-natured remark about the group's unwillingness to face important aspects of an issue.

Invite Outside Criticism. One of the dangers of groupthink is that information and communication from outside the group are often ignored or discounted. Any group in a financial institution can benefit from soliciting and then discussing criticism or suggestions from sources outside the group: other departments, customers, management, former employees, competing institutions. Such outside input might become a regular part of each group's meeting schedule.

Think Through Ideas Several Times. It is helpful to review goals, plans and decisions after enough time has passed for them to be judged objectively. Such "second looks" allow group members to examine the goals and ideas and more carefully consider the pros and cons of their effects on the group.

Break into Smaller Groups. On major tasks or important issues, it can be helpful to break the group into subgroups and let each of these discuss the task or tackle the issues. Such an approach may not eliminate groupthink; instead, it may result in a number of separate groups with groupthink problems. However, when the larger group is again reassembled, it will have a variety of alternatives to consider, and some of the dangers of groupthink can be minimized.

Summary

A major part of business communication takes place in group settings. Consequently, understanding the composition and dynamics of groups can enhance your communication skills at work. Organizations such as financial institutions include both formal groups that are sanctioned by the organization, and informal groups that are formed by individuals to satisfy common needs, interests or concerns.

All groups share four common characteristics: cohesiveness, individual/shared goals, norms and roles. Cohesiveness is group loyalty that results when members share and work toward common goals, operate with the same norms and feel comfortable with their roles in the group. Goals are what draw people into any group—both the individual objectives of each member and the goals that the group seeks to accomplish. Norms are unwritten values and beliefs about how group members should behave toward one another. Roles define patterns of behavior expected of individual members of the group. Two types of roles that exist in every group are task roles, which facilitate the group's effort to accomplish its goals, and maintenance roles, which help to foster smooth relationships among members.

Communication is most effective among members of cohesive groups. Consequently, it is possible to facilitate better group communication by building a strong sense of group cohesiveness. Groups can strengthen their cohesiveness by identifying and regularly reviewing goals, clarifying norms, and making certain that group members know and feel comfortable about their roles within the group.

Three common barriers to effective group communication are conflict, agendas and groupthink. Conflict can be healthy if it provides group members an opportunity to clarify problems or resolve differences, but it can also divert the group from its goals and destroy communication. You can minimize the dangers of negative group conflict by acknowledging the individual differences that are normal in any group, by remaining open-minded, by practicing good listening skills, by using empathy, and by using group goals, norms and roles to intercept and redirect personality conflicts.

Agendas are established procedures that outline processes to follow in order to reach goals. When handled with flexibility and a sensitivity to the feelings and moods of the group, agendas provide an invaluable framework for group communication. However, if agendas become too rigid or are followed slavishly, they can thwart creativity and communication among group members.

Groupthink—the negative side of group cohesiveness—is the tendency of highly cohesive groups to conform to "whatever the group wants." Groupthink can result in two communication problems: group members become reluctant to criticize or disagree with anyone else in the group, and individuals accept any group proposals as good without examining them. You can guard against groupthink by being open to and encouraging constructive disagreement among members, by inviting regular evaluation and criticism from sources outside the group, by taking regular "second looks" at group goals and decisions, and by breaking into smaller subgroups to examine major tasks or important issues.

Chapter Questions

1. According to this text, what is the definition of a group? Explain the two major kinds of groups and give two examples of each.
2. List and briefly explain the four characteristics of groups.
3. What is group cohesiveness? Why is cohesiveness important for group communication?
4. Explain the difference between individual and shared goals, and give an example of each from a formal group in a financial institution.
5. Describe the purpose of task and maintenance roles in group interaction.
6. Name four task roles and four maintenance roles in a group, and briefly explain the function of each.
7. Explain how shared goals and norms and clearly defined roles contribute to a group's cohesiveness.
8. How can role vacuums and role competition destroy cohesiveness in a group? Describe a strategy for dealing with role vacuums and role competition.

9. Define effective conflict, hidden agenda and groupthink, and explain how each can create barriers to group communication.

10. Describe two techniques for overcoming the communication barriers of conflict, hidden agenda and groupthink.

Footnotes

1. Brian L. Hawkins and Paul Preston, *Managerial Communication* (Santa Monica, Calif.: Goodyear, 1981), p. 163.

2. Albert C. Kowitz and Thomas J. Knutson, *Decision Making in Small Groups: The Search for Alternatives* (Boston: Allyn & Bacon, 1980), p. 98.

3. Solomon E. Asch, "Effects of Group Pressure upon the Modification and Distortion of Judgments," in H. Guetzkow, ed., *Groups, Leadership and Men* (Pittsburgh: Carnegie Press, 1951), pp. 177–190.

Hank Walker, Life Magazine © Time Inc.

"First learn the meaning of what you say, and then speak."

Epictetus
Discourses *(55- c.135 A.D.)*

10 Communication Applications

Objectives

After reading this chapter, you should be able to:

- Apply communication concepts and techniques presented in earlier chapters;
- Recommend appropriate solutions to communication problems.

IN PREVIOUS CHAPTERS, you learned about the communication process and ways that messages can be transmitted between people, either effectively or ineffectively. You also learned about the importance of communicating well and how it can improve your personal and professional life. Previous chapters identified the skills needed to communicate well in a variety of situations with co-workers, managers and customers. Applying this knowledge to your own experiences is the most effective way to reinforce the concepts learned and to improve your communication skills. An alternative to learning through real experiences is to study and analyze case studies. The following four case studies give you an opportunity to practice some techniques that can help make on-the-job communication more effective. As you read and analyze each situation, think about the communication techniques suggested in previous chapters as well as your own experiences. Use this knowledge to answer the questions at the end of each case study.

Case Study 1: Actions Speak Louder than Words

If you look closely at the person speaking, you may perceive a message contradicting the spoken message. Usually a verbal message is sent along with a nonverbal one. Someone may assure you that your visit is welcome, but their nonverbal communication—a nervous glance at the clock—indicates otherwise. People who can recognize and interpret nonverbal behavior increase their ability to understand messages. Consider the specific verbal and nonverbal communication problems in this case study and suggest ways that the participants might solve those problems.

Hometown Federal Savings, an institution with $200 million in assets, is located in a small, prosperous town in the Midwest. Hometown Federal has a sound loan portfolio, an experienced loan staff and good underwriting standards. In general, the institution has many satisfied customers who, once they have opened an account, remain loyal to the institution.

Like most financial institutions, Hometown Federal wants to attract new customers while retaining its current customer base. It has introduced a new product, the Fed-One Account, that combines the advantages of free checking, a high-yield money market account and a major credit card in one account. Employees have been instructed to offer this new account to every current and new customer to ensure their continuing relationship with the institution. Through studies, the institution has learned that the more accounts a customer has with an institution, the more likely the customer will continue to do business with the institution.

On a busy Friday afternoon, Ben Kowalski, a retired attorney, entered Hometown Federal and glanced quickly around the lobby. Mr. Kowalski is a long-time customer who comes into the institution regularly, spending time talking about his experiences as a trial attorney. Although many employees find his talks interesting, Mr. Kowalski often hinders the tellers' work and annoys many of the waiting customers. When his favorite teller is busy, Mr. Kowalski often visits the new accounts desk and tells Carrie Harrington his anecdotes.

Carrie was sorting through several new Fed-One Account applications as Mr. Kowalski approached her desk. It had been a tiring day and the last thing she needed was an hour of Ben Kowalski's "war stories." Carrie looked up while continuing to arrange the applications, grimaced and said, "Hello, Mr. Kozlowski. May I help you with something today?"

Mr. Kowalski frowned and growled: "That's Kowalski. Why don't you people ever get my name right? Don't you know who I am?"

Carrie sighed, rolled her eyes and leaned back in her chair: "Of course I know who you are, Mr. Kowalski. I'm sorry I mispronounced your name. What can I help you with?"

Mr. Kowalski shifted his weight from his right foot to his left and back again, looked around the lobby, straightened his tie and sat on the edge of the chair in front of the desk. As he placed his briefcase on Carrie's desk, the phone rang. Mr. Kowalski frowned and settled back into the chair as Carrie turned to answer the phone.

Carrie took a deep breath, rubbed her nose and said: "Carrie Harrington. Who? Oh, sure, Mrs. Hansen, I'd be happy to open a Fed-One Account for you. Could you come in to sign the application today? No, we're not too busy. I'll look forward to seeing you at three o'clock."

Carrie glanced at the clock and her watch as she hung up the phone. She shifted forward in her chair and looked dully at Mr. Kowalski: "So, now what did you want, Mr. Kowalski?"

Mr. Kowalski replied: "I want some information about your new Fed-One Account. You know, Ms. Harrington, I have a lot of money in this institution and I want to earn something on my investments."

Carrie shuffled through the papers on her desk for an application. When she couldn't find one, Carrie excused herself and walked to another desk for an application. On the way back to her desk, Carrie stopped for a drink of water and chatted for a few minutes with Martin Beck, a teller who was taking his break. As she spoke with Martin, Carrie twisted her gold pendant and pulled at her short skirt. Carrie smiled at Martin, leaned forward to whisper something in his ear and glanced over at her desk; then they both laughed. Mr. Kowalski was pacing in front of the desk. Carrie patted Martin's arm and returned to her desk. As Carrie sat down, Ben Kowalski also returned to the edge of his chair. He looked toward Martin Beck and shook his head.

"Well, Mr. Kowalski, here's the application. Would you like this to be an individual or a joint account?"

Ben Kowalski leaned forward, drummed his fingers on the desk and said loudly: "I'd like to learn a bit more about this account before I fill anything out. You know, I've been an attorney for many years. When you've seen all that I have, you learn to be cautious before you sign anything. Have I ever told you about the *Denver* v. *Billings* case?"

Carrie rested her chin in her right hand as Mr. Kowalski launched into a detailed description of the case. After five minutes, Carrie began to organize the papers scattered over her desk. After she arranged the applications in alphabetical order, Carrie looked at her computer screen, which displayed her daily appointments. She suddenly realized that she scheduled Mrs. Hansen and Ms. Coleman for the same time. Carrie located Mrs. Hansen's phone number and reached for her phone.

"I'm sorry to interrupt your story, Mr. Kowalski, but I need to make a phone call."

After Carrie rescheduled Mrs. Hansen, she said: "Now, did you want to discuss the advantages of the Fed-One Account, Mr. Kowalski? You know, we're offering this account to our preferred customers and you're certainly here enough to qualify for that status. So, can we get down to business?"

Ben Kowalski rubbed his chin, cleared his throat and stated: "You seem to be all business today, Carrie."

Carrie nodded: "First Federal is really pushing these Fed-One Accounts. The applications take a long time to complete and all our customers seem to want one. I already have a ton of these applications to process before I go home tonight, and more customers are coming in today."

"Well, that certainly isn't my fault, is it? After all, I am a valued customer of this institution. You know, Carrie, I've been with First Federal since before you were born. I knew Covington Tyson, the first president of this institution. Did I ever tell you about the time. . . ."

Carrie stared at the light fixture over her desk as Mr. Kowalski began his story. She had heard this story at least five times. As Carrie scratched her forehead and yawned, she looked at the clock. Mr. Kowalski had been at her desk for 20 minutes and Ms. Coleman was due in a few minutes. Carrie shrugged her shoulders, slumped in her chair and began to doodle on Mr. Kowalski's Fed-One application.

Ms. Coleman entered the lobby and walked toward the new accounts desk. Carrie smiled, removed her glasses and stood: "Good afternoon, Ms. Coleman. I see you're here for your three o'clock appointment. If you'll wait just a moment, I'll be happy to help you."

Ben Kowalski quickly rose from the chair, extended his hand to Ms. Coleman and said in a loud voice: "Nice to see you again, Ms. Coleman. I hope you have better luck with Ms. Harrington than I did. She wanted me to open a Fed-One Account. I've been waiting all afternoon, but she never got around to helping me. Guess she just can't handle complicated paperwork."

Carrie threw her hands in the air and sunk into her chair as Mr. Kowalski left the lobby.

Questions for Thought and Discussion

1. Nonverbal communication can aid or hinder communication. Describe at least one nonverbal cue that Carrie Harrington gave to communicate the following messages:

   a. I'm busy and don't have time to listen to you.

   b. I'm uncomfortable in this situation.

   c. I must end our discussion.

   d. Your financial needs concern me.

   e. You are important to me and my institution.

2. Put yourself in Ben Kowalski's position. Assume that you are anxious to learn about the institution's new product. In your opinion, what nonverbal messages were sent to you when the new accounts manager displayed each of the following behaviors?

   a. She remained seated at her desk when you entered her work area.

   b. Although she greeted you by name, she mispronounced your name and continued with paperwork as she said hello.

   c. She constantly looked at the clock, the ceiling or co-workers as she spoke with you.

   d. She smiled at co-workers as she spoke to you.

   e. Her desk was cluttered and she had to ask co-workers for supplies.

3. Carrie Harrington and Ben Kowalski are not strangers. Because they already have some expectations about each other, they could have used nonverbal cues more productively.
   a. Describe two ways Ben Kowalski might have helped Carrie Harrington understand the importance of his visit to the institution through nonverbal cues.
   b. Describe two ways Carrie Harrington might have steered Ben Kowalski toward opening a Fed-One Account by using nonverbal cues.
   c. Recommend two ways that each might have used paralanguage to enhance communication.
4. Personal space zones expand and contract, depending upon individuals' relationships. Explain how Carrie Harrington might have altered her public, social, personal and intimate zones to communicate various messages to Ben Kowalski, Martin Beck and Ms. Coleman.

Case Study 2: Crisis at Midland Bank

Listening skills are essential to the successful operation of businesses. When employees don't listen or don't listen well, feelings among employees and relationships with customers suffer. But, as you know from experience, it isn't always easy to listen effectively. The following case study illustrates how a combination of events, attitudes and feelings can block listening and result in an embarrassing situation. As you read the case study, consider ways Maria might have overcome some of the barriers to listening by using effective listening techniques.

Maria Toledano could feel the beginnings of a throbbing headache. She was ready to go home, take two aspirins and crawl into bed—but it was only nine-thirty in the morning.

Maria has been head teller at Midland Bank for two years. On most days, she loves her job—likes her co-workers, enjoys working with money and appreciates the interaction with customers. But not today.

This morning Maria arrived early, as usual, to check the teller stations and make sure everyone was stocked with plenty of cash. Today was the third of the month. Half of Midland's retiree customers would be coming in to deposit their Social Security checks or, if they had direct deposit, would be calling to make sure their checks had been credited to their accounts. Since this was also the end of the quarter, lots of people would be requesting updates on interest. The tellers would be swamped; they didn't need the added inconvenience of running out of cash.

Maria finished her rounds of the teller stations by nine o'clock, just as the bank opened its doors for business. Then two things happened almost at once: the teller terminals went down, and one of her best tellers called in sick. Maria quickly alerted her tellers to the problem with the terminals, telling them to process transactions by hand while she notified the computer service. After reporting the problem, she spent ten minutes on the phone lining up a part-time teller to fill in for the day.

By nine-thirty, the substitute teller was at his station. But the terminals were still down, and the lines of customers were ten deep. Most of these customers were retirees who wanted information about their deposits and interest—information that wasn't available because the terminals were down. Maria took a deep breath and began to move from teller station to teller station, fielding customer complaints and apologizing for the problem. "As if we can do anything about it," she muttered to herself.

In the middle of all this, Floyd Washington, the new accounts counselor, came by with a new customer. Maria was going through her tenth apology about the terminals when she saw Floyd approach. He stopped just on the other side of the customer counter and smiled nervously as he waited for her to finish. The new customer stood back several feet, scowling at the long lines and harried tellers. Maria's headache began throbbing in earnest. "Just what I need now," she thought.

Maria knew she was frowning as she turned toward Floyd, but she couldn't help herself. The man was really getting on her nerves. He'd been with the institution for four months, but he still wasn't getting the hang of his job. He kept sending customers to tellers with questions he should be answering, and his new account forms were invariably incomplete or incorrect. "Now what does he want?" Maria thought irritably.

"Yes? May I help you, Mr. Washington?" Maria rested an elbow on the counter and then turned and offered a stiff smile to the new customer.

"Uh, this is Mrs. Schreiner," Floyd said. "Mrs. Schreiner, this is Miss Toledano, our head teller. I think she can answer your questions."

Floyd was really nervous, Maria noticed. He kept glancing at the lines of customers and shifting a file folder from one hand to the other. The new customer stared at the lines as Floyd talked.

"Uh, Mrs. Schreiner just moved here from Murphysville,"

he went on, "and she wants to open an account with us. She's also shopping around for houses and would like information about our mortgage rates."

Maria managed to hold her frozen smile, but she glared at Floyd. "Great," she thought, "so you bring her to see me. I've got all the time in the world just now to answer questions about accounts—and our mortgage rates!"

As Floyd continued, Maria stared past him and watched a noisy interchange between the substitute teller and an angry customer. Following Maria's stare, Mrs. Schreiner began watching the same disturbance.

"Actually, the reason I've brought Mrs. Schreiner to see you, Miss Toledano," Floyd stammered, "is because she's concerned about all the—uh—confusion this morning. I told her we don't usually have this kind of a problem with customers. Well, not that the *customers* are the problem, really." Floyd laughed nervously. "I mean, well, I thought you might be able to explain."

Maria noticed that Floyd had stopped talking, and she shifted her glance back to him. She decided she'd have to deal with him quickly; the substitute teller was obviously in need of help. Maria tried to keep the irritation out of her voice as she spoke. "Well, Mr. Washington," she said, "I would be only too happy to explain about our accounts. But I wonder if you don't have all that information yourself? As you know, we *do* have brochures that list features of all our accounts. They were designed specifically for the use of new accounts counselors. And, actually, I'm not the person to ask about mortgage rates. Why don't you take Mrs. Schreiner over to Mrs. Larson in Residential Mortgage Lending? I'm sure she could answer your questions."

Maria smiled and nodded at the new customer. "Nice to have met you, Mrs. Schreiner. I'm sure you'll be pleased with any of our accounts, and I'm sure you'll find Mrs. Larson happy to answer your questions about our mortgage rates. Now, if you'll excuse me...we're having some problems this morning."

As Maria hurried away, Floyd Washington stared helplessly after her. Mrs. Schreiner also watched Maria's hasty departure. Several minutes later, Mrs. Schreiner turned down Floyd's offer to introduce her to the lending department, returned the forms for opening a new account and walked out of Midland Bank.

Questions for Thought and Discussion

1. The situation described in this case study presents a real challenge to communication. Briefly describe three ways Maria demonstrated effective communication skills.

2. Now focus on listening skills in the interchange involving Maria Toledano, Floyd Washington and Mrs. Schreiner. Using information from Chapter 5, find an illustration from the case study for each of the following barriers to effective listening. Briefly explain how each barrier interfered with Maria's ability to listen to Floyd Washington.

   a. physical barrier

   b. personal concerns

   c. false assumptions

   d. listener bias

   e. negative emotional state

3. Because of all these barriers, Maria failed to listen effectively to Floyd Washington. Consequently, she responded inappropriately and offended both Floyd and Mrs. Schreiner. Explain how the following strategies might have helped Maria to be a more effective listener.

   a. *Prepare your surroundings.* What could Maria have done to cope with the counter that separated her from Floyd and Mrs. Schreiner, the lines of impatient customers, and the disturbance at the one teller window?

   b. *Shift from speaker to listener.* How could Maria have prepared herself to focus on Floyd and the new customer?

   c. *Observe nonverbal cues.* What nonverbal cues from both Floyd and Mrs. Schreiner might have enabled Maria to listen more effectively?

   d. *Use empathy and objectivity.* How could an empathic, objective attitude have affected Maria's approach and reactions to both Floyd and Mrs. Schreiner?

Case Study 3: Friendly Persuasion

How many times did you attempt to persuade someone during the past week? You may have asked a customer to sign up for a new service, or asked a co-worker to help you work on a special project. Perhaps you asked your manager to provide additional resources to your department. You may have even asked your manager to send you to a special seminar . . . or requested a raise or a promotion!

Persuasion is pervasive in business. The following case illustrates the successful persuasion attempts of one department. As you read the case, identify the persuasion techniques that were presented in Chapter 6.

Ruby Smith's View

I've been in check processing for about 14 months now. Before that, I was a receptionist. I wanted to move to this department because I'm interested in getting more involved in the business—and to do that, you have to be part of operations.

This department is good to work in—we're busy and seldom have any downtime because checks are always coming in that must be processed. What we do is important—a lot of different areas depend on our work, and so do our customers.

Providing good customer service is important in this company, so we have to be accurate and efficient. Regulations limit the amount of time in which the institution must clear a check, so getting our work done on time is also important.

But the best thing is that management does what it can to help us get our work done. Here's an example of what I mean. Until this month, we had to use the photocopy machine in the records department. It was inconvenient because we would have to carry all of our materials over there to make copies. The people in records make lots of copies, too, so we would often have to wait a long time to use the machine. It was a bad situation for both departments.

This problem came up at a department meeting last April. Our supervisor, Mae Potempa, was going over our reports from the previous months. We had missed several deadlines and didn't even catch up after some overtime. Mae asked us to suggest ways to avoid these problems in the future.

I mentioned that I had spent a lot of time recently trying to get my copying done—and pretty soon we were talking about the problem. A couple of people who had been in the department for a long time said that the amount of copying they had to do was higher than it ever was before. I remember that one person—Ted—said that it wasn't worth talking about because we didn't have any chance of getting things changed. I guess we were all a little cautious because we knew that this whole organization is working on a tight budget. But Mae seemed interested, so a couple of us kept talking about how things could be better if we didn't have to face this obstacle.

We asked Mae if she would ask to have a photocopy machine for our own department. Mae said that she would, but only if we would help her show why one is needed. Most of us were very interested in seeing what we could do because we know that Mae does stand up for us.

One of my co-workers, Rosa, thought it would be a good idea to keep records of the amount of copies we need to make to do our work. And since we usually need to make copies right away rather than waiting to copy large batches, we decided to record the time of day, too. We also thought it would be a good idea to record whether we had to wait to use the machine and how long we waited. To have complete information, we agreed that everyone would have to keep this record. Even those department members who didn't think we would get anywhere with our request agreed to keep records. Rosa said she would create a form we could use and I volunteered to help her.

We kept those records for two months. You wouldn't believe the number of copies we made and the time it had taken! Even we were surprised.

Mae used information from our records in a proposal that she wrote to her manager, asking for a photocopy machine to be installed in our department. I know she mentioned that the members of the department thought we could do a better job if we had better access to a photocopy machine.

As I understand it, our manager agreed with Mae and sent the request along to the division manager. We now have a new photocopy machine right here in the department.

I feel pretty proud about it because I remember that I brought it up at that department meeting and I had something to do with making the department better.

Mae Potempa's View

The photocopying incident is a good example of how complex management is. Let me explain what I mean.

Over the past year and a half, we have made several major changes in our check handling procedures. Some of these were caused by changes in regulations; others came about because of improvements we were making throughout our systems. On top of that, the volume of checks we were handling was increasing.

While we were making changes in our procedures, we were always pretty good about providing the staff with training. That was important, because it is easy for morale to suffer if people feel that they are expected to do something for which they haven't been prepared. On the whole I have a good staff. And I know they want to be proud of the work they do. That's why I always make sure they get the training they need to do their jobs well.

But I have to admit, even I was short-sighted concerning the photocopying demands. The changes we had instituted, combined with the increased volume, greatly increased the number of copies that my staff had to make. At the same time, the records department—that's where my staff had to go to make copies—had also increased their use of the machine.

This topic came up at our April department meeting. Ruby Smith brought it up. While we have one or two chronic complainers in the department, Ruby isn't one of them. I know that when she reports a problem, she has probably given it some real thought. As the conversation developed, I could see that photocopying was probably consuming much more time than I had thought.

I wanted to increase productivity in the department, and I could see that having a photocopy machine right here could be valuable. But I knew that I would have to present a solid case to my manager. Our association normally operates on a conservative budget, and this is a particularly lean year.

I would have to present the request to my manager. She is what you might call a "numbers person." When I bring her a proposal, I know that I have to have real numbers to back it up.

I told my staff that I would try to get a machine for our own use, and that I would need their help to do so. Rosa, who has worked with me for several years, suggested that the department track its photocopying activity. Rosa and Ruby developed a rather good form to use, and the department kept records for two months.

I can only remember one real problem in the process. For the first few days when we were using the forms, Ted, one of my employees, complained to me and to one or two co-workers that filling out the form was a pointless, time-consuming activity. Unfortunately, Ted had recently become quite a complainer, and I thought that he was having a negative impact on some of his co-workers. I had a brief meeting alone with him in which I reviewed the purpose of the activity. I told him that I saw his constant complaining as counterproductive and that I expected him to support this important department project. As far as I know, Ted ended his complaining and complied with my request.

About three months ago, I wrote the proposal asking for a photocopy machine for our department. In my proposal, I outlined how our current equipment did not adequately support our new procedures and increased volume. I emphasized the increase in productivity I expected to occur if staff time were no longer wasted in waiting to use the photocopy machine. To arrive at these calculations I relied heavily on the data that my department gathered.

My manager was very impressed with my report. In fact, all she did was write a brief note on my cover memo and submitted my proposal up the line! I passed her compliments along to my staff—since they had done so much of the work—and I was sure to let my manager know about their contributions. Actually, it is part of the culture of this company to listen to the people who do the job. I like that.

We found out that we were getting the machine about a month ago. The news was so well received, you would have thought that I had announced that everyone was getting a raise!

Questions for Thought and Discussion

1. a. How would you describe Ruby Smith's view of her company?

   b. In what ways have communication practices shaped that view?

2. The text described five types of power. Describe the various ways that different types of power were used in this case study.

3. In this case, the supervisor was successful in having her staff contribute to the final proposal for a photocopy machine. Would you classify their reaction to the supervisor's use of power as commitment, compliance or resistance? Explain your answer.

4. What qualities allowed the supervisor to persuade her staff? What qualities allowed her to persuade upper management?

5. The supervisor in this case was generous in sharing credit with her staff. Imagine that, instead, she took all credit for the suggestion for herself. How might this change her credibility with her staff?

6. One expert in persuasion techniques has said, "People act for their own reasons, not for yours." How is that theory demonstrated in this case?

Case Study 4: Conflict at Delta Savings

When working with large numbers of people, as you do in your job at your financial institution, conflicts arise almost daily. Some may be important, others inconsequential, but they all follow the patterns described in Chapter 7. Small conflicts sometimes underlie larger, more fundamental differences that need to be resolved. One of the toughest steps to conflict resolution is recognizing a conflict and understanding its origin. To hone your skills in identifying and comprehending conflicts, consider the following case study in light of what you have learned so far about conflict resolution and human communication.

Delta Savings Bank has just promoted Keisha Burroughs, who has worked as a teller for six years, to the position of teller supervisor. Other tellers had been in the running for the job, including Diane Reynolds. But Keisha was so well liked by the tellers and respected for her performance by her superiors that the new appointment was expected to go rather smoothly. Her manager, Harry Dubnick, felt that he made the right decision because, while he and Keisha hadn't seen eye-to-eye about everything, he respected her efficiency and dedication.

About two weeks after Keisha's promotion, she sent a memo to her employees describing a directive that had come down from Delta Savings' regional manager, stating that because of new data processing requirements, tellers would now be expected to prepare two cash drawer audits—one at midday for the data processing department and one at the end of the day for the bookkeeping department—instead of one. The tellers were upset by the extra work for a number of reasons, primarily because it would necessitate limiting the amount of attention they would be able to give their customers. Delta Savings had always made it a point, both in its advertising and its employee training, that the number one priority of the institution was to give personalized, unhurried attention to its customers, many of whom had been saving their money there for years. Now it seemed the company was saying just the opposite. The increased work would mean that fewer tellers would be available at peak traffic times. The tellers nominated Diane Reynolds to speak to Keisha and voice their concerns.

Diane didn't bother to make an appointment with Keisha to talk about the directive, because Keisha had always been accessible. When she worked as a teller, she always had time for a co-worker with a problem. Diane walked into Keisha's office and said, "Keisha, the other tellers and I are confused about the memo you sent today."

Keisha looked up to see who was speaking, then returned to work on the report that was on her cluttered desk. "Why? The memo was clear about the new policy."

Diane was a little put off. "Well, some of us were concerned about what the extra work would entail."

Keisha continued to work on the papers in front of her. "The work is necessary for the data processing department, Diane. Besides, a little extra work never hurt anybody."

Diane was starting to get upset about Keisha's offhanded manner. She moved from the front of Keisha's desk around the side and said, "But Keisha, when you were a teller, you agreed with us that the customer . . ."

Keisha looked up from her work sharply and turned to face Diane. "Don't think you can get away with that with me," she said angrily. "Just because I used to be a teller doesn't mean that I can grant you any favors. The directive that came from the regional manager was explicit in what is expected and, as supervisor, it's my job to see that it's carried out. Please, I don't have time to listen to your complaints right now. I'm working on something much more important."

Diane didn't say anything and walked out of the office. With what she was thinking, it was a good thing that she didn't talk. To Diane, it seemed that a little authority had changed Keisha from a congenial co-worker to a short-tempered, unsympathetic tyrant. Diane didn't want to go back to the other tellers with nothing to show for her efforts, so with her feelings still hurt from the meeting, she decided to talk to Keisha's manager, Harry, about the problem.

Luckily when she got to Harry's office, he had just gotten back from lunch and had the time to talk. Diane sat down and explained, "The other tellers and I are confused about the new cash drawer audits. We're afraid they'll take so much time that customers will begin to complain about the number of closed teller windows and the slowdown in service, especially at lunchtime."

"That's a valid concern," Harry said. "What did Keisha say when you talked it over?"

"Well, she literally threw me out of her office. She said that her only job was to make sure that the directives she gets are carried out and not listen to our problems. She told me that 'a little extra work never hurt anyone.' She didn't even listen to my complaints."

Harry placed his hands on his head and leaned back in his chair, as he usually did when faced with a new problem. He was concerned about Keisha's behavior. It seemed that she might have problems communicating with her employees and keeping morale up. He thought it might have been a mistake to promote her. He also considered the possibility that Diane was resentful of Keisha's promotion. In his mind, this was a problem of communication between employees, not a major organizational decision. He thought the best course of action was to force Keisha and Diane to listen to each other's concerns and figure out how to work together better; otherwise, he thought, every problem between Keisha and the tellers would end up in his office. He told Diane, "I think you and Keisha better figure this one out for yourselves."

To Diane, this was the second insensitive remark she'd heard from management about this issue, so the signal to her was clear: Delta was no longer interested in the concerns of either its customers or its teller staff. She never bothered to ask Keisha again about the problem. Instead, she reported to the other tellers the apparent indifference that management held for their concerns. Morale eroded noticeably among the customer service staff. Customers became upset about both the closed teller windows and unfriendly service, and began to take their deposit account business elsewhere.

Questions for Thought and Discussion

1. What types of conflict were present in the case study? Name each incident and the type of conflict involved.
2. How did nonverbal messages add to the conflict? Verbal messages?
3. In what instances was effective listening lacking?
4. What assumptions was each person—Keisha, Diane and Harry—applying to their view of the conflict?
5. Did Keisha and Diane follow the required steps of conflict resolution? What was omitted?
6. Was Keisha wrong to employ domination? If not, how should she have responded?
7. Did Harry effectively handle his responsibility for helping resolve the conflict? Why or why not?
8. Create a scenario with dialogue in which Keisha, Diane and Harry cooperate in resolving the conflict.

INDEX